Every Day
I Sing the Blues

Every Day
I Sing the Blues

──── The Story of ────
B. B. King
By David Shirley

An Impact Biography

Franklin Watts
A Division of Grolier Publishing
New York/London/Hong Kong/Sydney
Danbury, Connecticut

*B. B. King is the most popular and enduring performer
in the history of the blues. For almost fifty years,
he has brought the rich music of the Mississippi delta
to audiences around the world.*

Photographs copyright ©: David Redfern/Retna Ltd.: p.2; Adam Scull/Globe Photos,
Inc.: p.11; Louise and Raeburn Flerlage: pp.14, 61; Photofest: p.16; Mimosa
Records Productions, Inc.: p. 20; Charles Sawyer: pp. 24, 32, 34, 39, 46
(Courtesy of Mrs. Robert Henry), 79, 91; Michael Ochs Archives, Venice, CA.: pp.
49, 82, 93; Frank Driggs Collection: pp. 54, 63, 65 (both E. C. Withers), 68
(Larry Cohn); E. C. Withers/Mimosa Records Productions/Michael Ochs Archives,
Venice, CA.: p. 57; UPI/Bettmann: p. 71; Amalie R. Rothschild/The Bettmann
Archive: p. 86; Ernest C. Withers: pp. 104, 108; Gibson, USA: p. 109;
Reuters/Bettmann: p.112.

Library of Congress Cataloging-in-Publication Data

Shirley, David, 1955-
Every day I sing the blues : the story of B. B. King/by David Shirley.
p. cm.—(An Impact biography)
Includes bibliographical references (p.) and index.
Summary: Traces the life of the dedicated and talented blues musician,
from his birth in the Mississippi Delta in 1925 to the present.
ISBN 0-531-11229-2—ISBN 0-531-15752-0 (pbk.)
1. King, B. B.—Juvenile literature. 2. Blues musicians—United
States—Biography—Juvenile literature. [1. King, B. B.
2. Musicians. 3. Afro-Americans—Biography. 4. Blues (Music)]
I. Title.
ML3930.K46S55 1995
781.643'092—dc20
[B] 94-16151
CIP AC MN

Contents

Every Day
I Sing the Blues

The King
of the Blues

The date is January 15, 1992, and the banquet-hall stage at New York City's elegant Waldorf-Astoria Hotel is crowded with famous rock-and-roll guitarists. The occasion is the annual induction ceremony for the Rock and Roll Hall of Fame. Many of the most talented musicians in popular music have assembled to pay tribute to the legendary Les Paul, the man who pioneered the electric guitar and one of the evening's inductees. In an interview the day before the event, Ahmet Ertegun, the chairman of the Hall of Fame, described the lineup of guitarists for the program as "mind-boggling."[1] Few people attending the ceremony would argue with him.

Jeff Beck and Jimmy Page are here. During the 1960s and 1970s, the two popular British musicians lent their towering guitar solos to such groups as the Yardbirds, the Rod Stewart Band, and Led Zeppelin. Standing beside Beck and Page is Carlos Santana, a true guitar virtuoso and one of the first musicians to combine rock and roll with Latin rhythms and jazz-style improvisations. Toward the center of the stage stand two more rock superstars: the Rolling Stones' Keith Richard, rock and roll's most accomplished rhythm guitarist, and the Edge, the guitarist for the Irish rock ensemble U2. Lurking in the corner is Neil Young, one of popular music's most gifted songwriters. Over the years, Young has added his wild, thrashing guitar playing to the Buffalo Springfield, Crazy Horse, and Crosby, Stills, Nash and Young. Toward the back of the stage, Robbie Robertson, the lead guitarist and mastermind of the folk-rock ensemble, the Band, is strumming away on his guitar.

The most commanding figure on the stage, however, is a huge, dark-skinned man standing proudly at the center of the group—the great blues guitarist and vocalist Riley "B. B." King. At sixty-six, with his closely cropped hair speckled with gray, King is old enough to be the grandfather of many of the young rock-and-roll fans and musicians in the crowd. But he still plays and sings with an energy and enthusiasm that few of the younger musicians on the stage can equal.

Almost bursting out of his black tuxedo, King has bright, narrow eyes behind his tinted glasses and a warm, wide smile. At his side, he dangles a shiny red guitar. When his time comes to lead the group with a solo, King jerks the instrument to his chest and throws back his head with his eyes tightly closed. The crowd erupts with screams and applause as his large, stubby fingers flutter effortlessly across the neck of his guitar and a loud, piercing wail suddenly echoes throughout the hall.

King is at the Waldorf tonight to introduce his old friend and touring partner Bobby "Blue" Bland. After more than forty years as one of the most popular and durable of blues singers, Bland is finally being inducted into the Hall of Fame. The evening's other honorees include the Yardbirds, the Jimi Hendrix Experience, Sam and Dave, the Staple Singers, the Isley Brothers, and Booker T. and the MGs. King has not yet been elected to the prestigious club, but his importance among the group is secure. There is probably not a musician on the stage or in the audience at the Waldorf who has not been influenced in some way by his passionate singing and powerful blues guitar.

At an age when most people are thinking about retirement, B. B. King has just finished the best year of his career. He had several successful recordings during 1991, including a

B. B. King was proud to introduce his old friend and touring partner, Bobby "Blue" Bland, at 1992's Rock and Roll Hall of Fame induction ceremony in New York City.

long-awaited reunion with his friend Joe Sample and the Crusaders. He headlined a popular nationwide blues festival sponsored by Benson and Hedges, and was named blues artist of the year in a number of year-end readers' and critics' polls. He even fulfilled a lifelong ambition by opening his own music club, the Blues Bar, on the 20-block stretch of Beale Street in Memphis, Tennessee, where he first launched his career five decades earlier.

King has come a long way since his early days as a sharecropper in the Mississippi Delta. Each time he plays in front of a crowd like the one at the Waldorf, he thinks back on the stubborn dedication and endless hours of work that brought his music to national prominence.

After moving to Memphis in the late 1940s, King spent the early years of his adult life as a local disc jockey and radio musician, known to his fans as the "Beale Street Blues Boy." His career finally began to take off in the 1950s, as he performed almost every night of the year in the endless parade of southern beer halls and nightclubs known as the "chitlin circuit." By the late 1960s, King had become one of the most popular musicians in the world, a distinction he has held throughout the remaining years of his career.

Along the way, he has played in dozens of countries around the world, entertaining presidents, queens, and stadiums full of screaming rock-and-roll fans. He has also received almost every honor and award that a popular musician can earn, including the Presidential Medal of Honor—the highest honor available to a United States civilian.

With all his success and good fortune, however, King has never forgotten what it means to sing the blues. Anyone who has ever heard him sing and play the guitar can tell that the man has suffered a great deal during his life. In performance, his voice is a clear, piercing wail, and his short, restrained guitar solos sound—more than anything else—like sudden bursts of crying. People in the audience often cry themselves when they hear King perform, as they discover their own pain and loss in the sad, mournful story of the blues.

"The blues came about 'cause people have problems," King told an interviewer in 1986, "problems with money, problems with love—and as long as people have problems, people [are] gonna be playin' the blues. [The blues] doesn't paint the pretty pictures other music does—it gets down to the point, down to the music. The simplicity makes it real. The blues ain't no put-on," he concluded. "It tells you stories about real things."[2]

The blues has meant many things for King during his life. It meant being separated from his father at the age of four, when his mother suddenly took him from his childhood home. It meant facing his beloved mother's death when he was only nine, and years of backbreaking work and inescapable poverty on a Mississippi cotton plantation. It also meant sleeping in the back rooms of bars and hustling spare change on street corners as he first tried to establish himself as an entertainer. And it meant suffering through two failed marriages and constant separation from his children as he spent most of his adult life performing on the road.

More than anything else, however, the blues for B. B. King has meant being black. "I personally think," he told an interviewer in 1986, long after he had become successful, "that however wealthy you might be in this country—and I've been around the world four or five times and haven't found any country I would like to live in other than this one—being a black person, you've got to have the blues all your life."[3]

Surprisingly, given King's recent success, the blues also meant enduring for years the indifference of white music fans and, at times, the open hostility of young black people in his audiences. It still hurts him today that young white rock-and-roll fans accepted him and his style of blues years before many people in the African-American community.

"They said, 'Now we bring you B. B. King,'" he told *Rolling Stone* magazine in 1989, remembering how his flamboyance and showmanship embarrassed some black listeners in the 1960s and 1970s, "and everybody said, 'Boo!' Well, that hurt me very deeply."[4]

McKinley Morganfield, more commonly known as "Muddy Waters," was one of the powerful Mississippi Delta musicians who first inspired King to sing the blues.

It also bothers King that the younger men beside him on the stage tonight—like most young musicians who openly claim him as an influence—are all either white or Hispanic. He knows, of course, that there are many gifted young blues guitarists who are African-Americans, such as Robert Cray and Kenny Neal. During the past quarter of a century, however, the musicians who have truly followed in King's footsteps—guitarists like Eric Clapton, Bonnie Raitt, and Elvin Bishop—have predominantly been white. It was Bishop and his friend Mike Bloomfield, and not some successful black blues guitarist of the day, who first introduced King to rock-and-roll fans in the late 1960s as, "the big monster, B. B. King, the greatest living blues guitarist."[5]

Musicians like Bishop, Clapton, and Keith Richard have consistently been among King's most outspoken admirers and often gone out of their way to promote him and his music. A tour with Richard and the Rolling Stones in 1969 gave King his first real nationwide audience. And 20 years later, a similar tour with U2, along with a celebrated duet with the group's lead singer Bono, brought King the greatest exposure of his forty-five-year career.

King is grateful for the recognition he has received over the years from the white rock-and-roll establishment. He is always quick to repay the compliments of his younger white peers. It hurts the aging blues master, however, that his music was not first discovered by young black musicians.

"The point that has bothered me a lot," he once complained in an interview, "has been that many of the young white players that are playing the blues are admired and idolized by a lot of the young blacks. [Young black audiences] are not ashamed of that, but if it's me or some of the guys that traditionally did this all along, well, then the young blacks shied away from the blues."[6]

King has responded to this situation by playing every chance he gets for both white and black audiences. His live performances now include large concert halls, Las Vegas supper clubs, and occasionally even the White House. But he still spends a large part of each year traveling in his tour bus to

King and blues-rock legend Eric Clapton trade solos during a televised concert. Clapton, whose collaboration with John Mayall's Bluesbreakers made him a star during the London blues revival of the 1960s, was one of the first young guitarists to cite King as an influence.

smaller clubs and concert halls where he performs for black blues fans across the country.

Playing before so many different types of people has caused King to change certain things about his performing style and his song selection over the last few years. Some things have remained the same, however, particularly the guitarist's endless desire to please a crowd.

"The audience now is a much wider range of people," he told an interviewer a month after the Hall of Fame performance.

My association with U2 has brought even really young kids in to hear what I do. So I will do things now I probably wouldn't have done years ago, before I didn't know to do those things then. For instance, I survey each audience and see musically as well as visually how they take the tunes. So if I do a couple of tunes that get no real reaction, I shift to different lines. I've got to try and be a pleaser![7]

The audience at the Rock and Roll Hall of Fame ceremony is certainly pleased as King and his fellow guitarists complete their brief set. On the final note, all the guitars merge together into a huge blast of sound, as the crowd rises to its feet with a thunderous ovation. As the crowd continues to applaud, the musicians group together at the center of the stage to take a bow. King takes a moment to gaze around the hall at the appreciative crowd and the talented group of men beside him on the stage. He seems genuinely moved by the scene. He has clearly come a long way since the early days of his career, when he was booed frequently by small crowds on the chitlin circuit.

Even in the worst of times, however, King never liked to give up on an audience—even when the crowd seemed to hate his music. King's refusal to quit and his fierce determination to please have been the keys to his success over the years. He always believed that even the most unreceptive audience would eventually come around.

"I did a tune called 'Sweet Sixteen,' which is one of my big tunes," he said in 1989 about his early days playing for unreceptive audiences, "and there's a few lines in there that kind of pleased me, like getting it off my chest. 'Treat me mean, but I'll keep on loving you just the same/But one of these days, you'll give a lot of money/Just to hear somebody call my name.'"[8]

Music journalist Stanley Booth was in the audience one of those rough nights when King refused to give in to a hostile crowd. It was the summer of 1968, and King was playing the three A.M. show at the Club Paradise in Memphis. The joint was half-empty as King began his final set. Throughout the show, most of the crowd spent more time laughing and talking at their tables than listening to the music. On one occasion, a drunk actually jumped on the bandstand and tried to pull King off the stage.

King was determined to win the crowd's approval, however. Finally, toward the end of the set, he burst without warning into a loud, seemingly random series of guitar notes that drowned out everything else in the room. Behind him, the drummer and organist began to make a similar racket. With the audience's attention suddenly focused on the stage, he lurched with the rest of the band into a soul-wrenching version of his classic single, "Three O'Clock Blues." "It's three o'clock in the morning," he sang, as the women in the front began to scream. "Can't even close my eyes." By the time the song and the set had ended, everyone in the club was standing and applauding madly. One older woman toward the front was even dancing on her chair.

"I just want to make people happy," King told Booth shortly after the performance.

> Black, white, red or green. There are a lot of places I want to go and things I want to do, but if I can just go on playing my music for the people, that's enough. It's all I live for.[9]

How Blue
Can You Get?

The Mississippi Delta is known for two things: cotton and the blues. King Cotton, as the soft, white plant is often called by the locals, has been the area's main cash crop since the days of slavery. Stretching almost 200 miles (320 km) along the east banks of the Mississippi River—from the sprawling metropolis of Memphis at its northernmost point to the gently rolling hills of Vicksburg in the south—the Delta boasts some of the richest farmland in the world. Before the Civil War, white Mississippi landowners reaped great fortunes from the region's dark, fertile soil and the free, often back-breaking labor of the African slaves who worked the fields.

The scene has changed somewhat over the years. Sophisticated farm machinery can now do in minutes what it once took dozens of farmworkers an entire day to achieve, and crops such as soybeans and catfish have actually challenged cotton as the region's leading product.

Even with all the changes, however, cotton and those who own it still rule the Mississippi Delta. A handful of wealthy planters still occupy the huge cotton plantations that their ancestors built more than a century ago, and the distant descendants of slaves still plow the fields, plant the seeds, and harvest the crops beneath the blistering Mississippi sun.

For most people, the blues and the Mississippi Delta are

The mysterious Robert Johnson may have been the greatest of all the Delta bluesmen. Johnson's playing was so amazing, in fact, that some people believed he had acquired his talent in a deal with the devil.

practically one and the same. "It's the sharecropper," explains blues historian Larry Cohn, "the black man suffering in the noonday sun and moaning and singing and that kind of thing. I think there was a tremendous visual romance that came out of that kind of thing."[1]

Of course, the Mississippi Delta has not been the only region to claim gifted blues musicians over the years. During the 1920s and 1930s, classic blues singers, such as Bessie Smith, Ida Cox, and Gertrude "Ma" Rainey, took New York and Chicago by storm, while a new breed of Texas musicians, like Huddie "Leadbelly" Ledbetter and Blind Lemon Jefferson, helped popularize a quieter, folk-style blues throughout the Southwest.

But the sparsely populated Mississippi Delta has produced far more than its share of blues singers and composers over the years, including the majority of the tradition's most famous and influential musicians. In fact, a brief list of the area's most celebrated singers and guitarists reads like a "Who's Who" of the blues.

The two towering figures of country blues guitar spent their early lives working in the fields of the Delta. McKinley Morganfield, known to most of the world as "Muddy Waters," was born and raised in the great Stovall plantation just outside of Clarksdale. And the extraordinarily gifted Robert Johnson, who—according to local legend—acquired his rare musical talents in an ill-fated deal with the devil, grew up in the northern Delta town of Robinsonville.

Eddie "Son" House, a Baptist minister who successfully combined the techniques of the blues and gospel, spent most of his youth in the tiny village of Lyon in Coahama County. As a child, the great blues shouter Chester "Howlin' Wolf" Burnett toiled beside his parents in the deep rows of the Dockery plantation, near Ruleville. And though Charley Patton, the first Delta singer to capture the attention of the white-owned recording industry during the 1920s, was actually raised in the hill country between Jackson and Vicksburg, he migrated to the heart of the Delta the first chance he got.

The last of the great Delta blues musicians, Riley "B. B." King was born in a dilapidated wooden cabin just outside of Itta Bena on September 16, 1925. His childhood roughly spanned the period when the musicians mentioned above were beginning to make a name for themselves and the harsh, mournful music they were creating.

B. B.'s parents, Albert and Nora Ellen, had married the year before, after a brief courtship. Riley was to be the couple's first and only child. Like their parents before them, the Kings were trying to eke out a living as sharecroppers on another person's property. In the years before and during the Great Depression of the 1930s, sharecropping was a common, and miserable, way of life for poor farmers in the region.

For most poor farmers—black and white alike—sharecropping differed very little from the system of legalized slavery that preceded it. According to the normal agreement, the sharecropper received a small house in which to live, a few acres of modest farmland, and a few simple farming tools. The costs of seeds, fertilizer, and everything else that was needed to get the crop to market were shared equally with the white landlord, along with a fifty-fifty split of any profits that were generated by the harvest after all the other expenses had been paid.

Most years, conditions such as flooding or drought ensured a poor harvest, and the majority of farmers were rarely able to cover their basic expenses, much less earn a profit from their labors. On such occasions, landowners were usually willing to lend their tenants the money to survive the winter and cover their share of the costs for the next season's crop. But even with the landlord's generosity, sharecroppers were often left with a large debt that they could never fully repay. Under this system, thousands of hardworking farmers throughout the Deep South found themselves permanently bound to a tiny plot of land that they would never own, living under conditions of poverty and debt that they could never hope to overcome—at least through hard, honest work.

For many farmers, the only real solution was to run away, sometimes leaving behind their spouses and children along with their unpaid debts. Some simply moved on to farms in neighboring counties to try their hands at sharecropping once again, with no debts and a new identity. During the years of Riley's childhood, however, more and more people fled north—to midwestern cities like St. Louis, Kansas City, and Chicago—and the promise of wealth and racial equality that awaited them there.

After Riley's birth, his parents did their best to make ends meet. Whenever he had the opportunity, Albert King took time off from his farm chores to work double shifts driving a tractor on a nearby plantation. The pay was meager even for the time—only fifty cents for a full day's labor—but the family desperately needed the extra money to survive. Even with Albert's second job, however, the debts were simply too great. Finally, the King family—like so many other black Mississippi families during the period—began to come apart under the constant pressures of sharecropping.

One day, when Riley was only four years old, his mother took him to her parents' home in the neighboring town of Kilmichael in the hill country to the east. Still a teenager, Nora Ellen wanted to start her life again, free from the debts that the family had gathered in Itta Bena, and she left the farm suddenly, without telling her husband where she and her child were going. Another five years would pass before Riley and his father would communicate again.

A proud young woman who was determined to find a way to support her son, Nora Ellen would marry twice more during Riley's early childhood. Riley adored his mother, and for the next few years he lived for a brief time in the homes of both of his respective stepfathers. Both marriages were shaky from the start, however, eventually crumbling under the same economic pressures that had destroyed his parents' life together. Because his mother was unable to provide him with a stable family life, Riley spent most of his time in the home of his maternal grandmother, Elnora Farr.

Like her daughter, Riley's grandmother made her modest living as a sharecropper, and the two women also shared a devout faith in the Evangelical Christian religion that claimed the devotion of so many of the region's poor black farmers. Although Riley would later become famous playing and singing

King's childhood home is now dilapidated, but even at its best was simply a shack with a dirt floor. It was typical of the kind of poor conditions under which black people in Mississippi lived during the 1920s and 1930s.

the blues, his first musical experiences were in the black churches of the Mississippi Delta.

Both Riley's mother and grandmother were Baptists, and as a youngster he often attended Sunday services at the tiny black Baptist congregation in Kilmichael. Music had always played an important role in the King family. Riley's grandfather was a talented guitar player, and both his parents loved to sing. It was only after he made the acquaintance of his Uncle Archie Fair, however, that Riley really began to develop a passion for music—especially the music of black Pentecostal religion.

Archie Fair was a minister in the Pentecostal Holiness Church. In contrast to the more reserved form of worship practiced in the Baptist church where Riley's mother and grandmother attended services, the Holiness Church practiced a wilder, more spirited form of religion. It appealed to the poorest, most socially outcast members of the black community.

During a normal Pentecostal service, the members of the congregation were encouraged by the minister to let go of the pressures and worries of their everyday lives. Instead, they were instructed to submit themselves entirely to the guidance of the spirit of God, or the Holy Ghost.

Under the influence of the Holy Ghost, Pentecostal worshipers sometimes behaved very strangely. It was not unusual in Reverend Fair's services to hear people speak in languages that they had never heard before or to see an entire row of worshipers shake violently in their seats. Occasionally, a person would become so overwhelmed that he or she would actually faint and fall to the floor, right in the middle of the service. Others would lay on the floor and roll themselves up and down the aisles while the minister continued his sermon.

Pentecostal worshipers also produced glorious music under the spell of the Holy Ghost. Often accompanied by nothing more than a tambourine and the clapping of the other worshipers' hands, a soloist would shout out the inspiring verses of the songs. The message was always the same: the good news—or the gospel—of the love of Jesus, and the horrible judgment awaiting those who turned their backs on the gospel. When the singer finished a verse, the entire congregation would shout back the song's familiar chorus. With each new verse and each repeated chorus, the crowd would grow more and more excited, and their singing would become more and more inspired.

At the center of the service was the Reverend Archie Fair. Like other Pentecostal ministers, the Reverend Fair preached his sermons in a loud, rambunctious style meant to inspire the congregation and incite them to all sorts of outrageous behavior. At times, he would raise his powerful baritone voice to a thundering roar that would make the windows of the tiny wood-framed church house shudder. Throughout the sermon, he would stomp his feet, pound his fist on the pulpit, even dance around in front of the choir violently strumming the electric guitar that hung from his shoulder. And then, all at once, he would grow very still, dropping down on his knee and lowering his voice to a whisper. Sometimes he would speak so quietly that the worshipers had to strain their necks forward to hear what he was saying. And then—just when the entire hall had been reduced to silence—his powerful voice would erupt into a whole new round of shouting. Or he would break forth into the verse of a favorite hymn, with the choir and congregation quickly joining in on the chorus. Everyone was delighted by these services—and no one more than young Riley King.

Taken from his father when he was only four, and then shuffled back and forth between the homes of his mother and grandmother, Riley had become a very shy and awkward child. He often stuttered when he had to speak in public. After his mother's death, Riley's shyness became even worse. He had little enthusiasm for activities at school or his studies, and he withdrew even further into himself and away from the other children in the community.

In many ways, a Pentecostal worship service was the perfect place for a shy, lonely little boy. Caught up in the excitement of the service, Riley forgot about himself and his problems. He got lost in the power of his uncle Archie's preaching and the glorious music of the choir and the congregation.

It was also during these lively Pentecostal services that Riley first discovered that he had a special gift for music. Although he often stuttered when he talked, Riley's singing was pure and uninterrupted. In fact, his young tenor voice was already so strong and clear that he quickly gained the attention, and the praise, of his elders—particularly his uncle Archie. The Reverend Fair insisted that it was the Holy Ghost who sang so beautifully through Riley's throat whenever the youngster joined in with the choir.

Riley did not know why he sang so easily and so well. All he knew was that it felt good to sing in church. He loved to rear back his head and let his clear tenor voice fill the room. After he discovered his talent for singing, Riley went to church with his uncle Archie every chance he got. By the time he was ten years old, he was a regular soloist with the choir and he frequently led the entire congregation in singing.

Riley was also fascinated by the Reverend Fair's electric guitar. During the services, the boy watched with awe as the older man furiously strummed the instrument to create a bright, piercing sound that filled the hall with excitement. Whenever the Reverend Fair went out to visit the members of his congregation, Riley would pull the large wooden guitar out from under the minister's bed. At first, Riley was frustrated with the bulky instrument; no matter how hard he tried, he simply could not reproduce the magical sounds he heard his uncle play in church. But the Reverend Fair recognized how serious his nephew was about learning to play the guitar. He taught Riley the E-A-B chord progression on which most gospel and blues songs were based. "I learned three chords [from him]," Riley would remember years later, "but those three have stayed with me through the years."[2] Armed with this new information, Riley practiced the guitar constantly, often neglecting his schoolwork and chores. Before long, however, all the hard work had begun to pay off, and he could play the instrument even better than his uncle Archie.

Riley did not realize it at the time, but he would one day have to choose between gospel music and the blues. Although the two traditions shared many things in common, they also appealed to different segments of the African-American community of the Mississippi Delta.

Gospel songs were normally sung in church, usually by the entire congregation. The music was lively and joyous, and the lyrics boasted happily of the new life that the believer had found in the church. The gospel singer had also rejected all the worldly vices—the drinking, gambling, drugs, and sexual obsessions—that ruined the lives of so many poor black people.

The blues, on the other hand, were normally sung in beer halls and juke joints, most often by a solitary individual crouched sadly over an acoustic guitar. Where gospel singers boasted of their purity, blues singers bragged unashamedly about their wild lives and worldly adventures. And where gospel songs were happy and optimistic, the blues were openly mournful. Blues songs were often peopled with drifters, drug addicts, and drunks. More than anything else, they told the tragic stories of men and women whose hearts had been broken by an unfaithful lover—or whose lovers had left them for their own infidelity.

Riley was not the only blues singer to be inspired by the spirited music of the black Pentecostal church. By the time he began singing in the choir of his uncle Archie's church in the early 1930s, older blues musicians like Son House, Charley Patton, Muddy Waters, and John Lee Hooker were already combining elements of gospel and the blues in their performances. And there were plenty of fans throughout the South who loved to hear the "holy blues" they played. Few of these fans, however, were churchgoers. For most black Christians in the Mississippi Delta, gospel and the blues simply could not be mixed. Those who chose to sing the blues, insisted many black Christians of the day, chose to leave the church and its music behind.

"The blues make you lie," the great rhythm-and-blues shouter "Little" Richard Penniman would instruct his fans two decades later, shortly after his own conversion from singing the blues. "The blues make you cry about somebody else's wife, about somebody else's husband. The blues make you make phone calls you can't pay for. Do you think God wants you to have the blues? God don't want you to have no blues!"

After his mother's death, Riley continued to live with his grandmother on the farm near Kilmichael. When he could take the time from his sharecropping duties, he attended the tiny one-room schoolhouse run by the local Baptist church in nearby Elkhorn. Since most of the other schoolchildren were also needed on the farm, the school year lasted for only the five or six months between the fall harvest and planting in the spring.

Riley was never a very serious student. He preferred the worship services at his uncle Archie's church and the time he spent practicing his guitar to classrooms and homework. But Riley's teacher at the Elkhorn School, a man named Luther Henson, played an important role in the young man's life. A proud, determined man, Henson tirelessly preached a message of positive thinking and self-improvement to the poor farm children who crowded the Elkhorn classroom. He taught his pupils that nothing—not even the poverty and racism that they encountered every day—should be able to keep them from realizing their dreams. If they worked hard enough and long enough, he insisted, they could achieve any goal. To prove his point, he read his classes the poetry and prose of black American writers such as Phillis Wheatley, Harriet Tubman, and Paul Laurence Dunbar. Each of these people, Henson told his students, had overcome ignorance and poverty to produce works of great beauty and power.

Henson also introduced his students to the *Black Dispatch*, an African-American weekly newspaper published in Oklahoma City. Inside the paper were photographs of contemporary black celebrities like Joe Louis, Jesse Owens, and Louis Armstrong. The pictures in the *Black Dispatch* had a profound impact on Riley. If these people could escape poverty and make something special of their lives, he reasoned, then perhaps he could, too.

The classroom was not the only place where Riley learned about the significant achievements of black Americans. Through his mother's sister Jemima, he was first introduced to the blues and the popular musicians who would soon play such an important role in his life. "She was like a teenager today who would buy all the records of various performers," he said of his aunt Jemima many years later.

> How she learned about them, I don't know. This was when I was about eight or nine, perhaps even younger. She would let me play the Victrola, let me wind it up. I would hear what she would play, but when I played it, I could pick my favorites.[3]

Listening to his aunt Jemima's record collection, Riley first heard the music of gospel legend Reverend Gates and great blues singers such as Lonnie Johnson, Bukka White, and Sonny Boy Williamson. "Sonny Boy Williamson," King said remembering the great blues harmonica player, "when I was a teenager, I was crazy about him."[4]

Riley's family was too poor to afford a radio at the time. And even when he did get the chance to listen to the radio, there were very few local stations that played music made by or for black people. As he grew older, however, he heard more recordings by popular black artists on the nickel jukeboxes of the black cafés and diners of Kilmichael and Indianola. Occasionally, he even caught a glimpse of some of his musical heroes in action.

"In Indianola, they had one nightclub called Johnny Jones' Nightspot," he later remembered, "and I would see many popular artists of the day there. It had holes in the side, so although us kids couldn't get in, we could see the performances. We'd see how they would dress, how they'd carry themselves, and what kind of automobiles they'd come in."[5]

The cars and fancy clothes made a deep impression on a young boy too poor to afford his own guitar. At times, Riley tried with little success to build his own instrument. One early attempt featured a single string—a piece of wire borrowed from a broken broom—stretched tightly between two nails on the side of his house. Riley would use a bottle or a kitchen knife to make the strings squeal like a slide guitar.

On January 15, 1940, Riley's grandmother died after a long battle with tuberculosis. Elnora Farr had worked hard her entire life, but she was still in debt to her white landlord at the time of her death. At fourteen years of age, Riley was left penniless and alone. For a few months, he was shuffled back and forth between the homes of relatives and friends in the area. Finally in the fall, Riley moved to the Delta town of Lexington to live with his father. For ten years, Riley had desperately missed his father, and he was happy at first to become a part of Albert King's new family. But music had already become the biggest part of Riley's life. In Lexington, he was expected to spend all his time working on the farm. There were few opportunities to make or listen to music. Riley especially missed singing in the Pentecostal church choir and playing his uncle Archie's guitar. After two years in his father's home, Riley packed a small bag and rode his rusty old bicycle over the 50 miles (80 km) of gravel roads from Lexington to Kilmichael.

Riley was seventeen years old when he arrived back in Kilmichael. The clothes he was wearing were torn and tattered. He had no job, no money, and no place to stay. Flake Cartledge, a local white tenant farmer who had known Riley's mother, took pity on the youngster. He gave Riley some new clothes, a place to stay in the storage shed outside his house, and a job doing small chores on his farm. Cartledge also loaned Riley $2.50 to buy a used guitar, and the young man formed his first gospel singing group along with cousin Birkett Davis, his close friend Walter Doris, and some other young men from the surrounding farms.

When Birkett Davis moved to Indianola later in the year, he discovered that he could earn much higher wages working on the large cotton plantations in the heart of the Delta. It took very little to persuade Riley to join his cousin on the new job site. Birkett lent Riley the money to repay Flake Cartledge for the cost of the guitar, and the two young men cruised out of

31

By the time Riley moved to Lexington to live with his father,
music was already the most important thing in his life. This
photo was taken by a storefront photographer in nearby
Indianola, when Riley was sixteen.

Kilmichael in a car that Birkett had borrowed from a friend in Indianola.

Riley, who was now eighteen, quickly found a job driving a tractor for a dollar a day on the Barrett plantation, just outside of Indianola. He began dating a local girl named Martha Denton, and both he and Birkett joined a gospel singing group, a five-man chorus called the Famous St. John Gospel Singers. With Riley accompanying the group on guitar, the young men gained a local following by imitating other popular groups of the day, like the Golden Gate Quartet and the Dixie Hummingbirds. The group started off singing in local churches and community centers. They soon became so popular, however, that Riley and his friends were frequently performing live broadcasts on WGRM, a local radio station in Greenwood.

When not performing with his friends, Riley also made extra money playing blues on the street corners of Indianola. But at eighteen, gospel music was still his first love, and he dreamed of making a name for himself with his new singing group. "I didn't think that I would be a blues singer," Riley later told an interviewer. "That's far from what I thought. I thought I would be popular, but as a gospel singer."[6]

Convinced that the Famous St. John Gospel Singers were good enough to appeal to a much larger audience, Riley began trying to persuade his friends to quit their jobs on the plantation and seek their fame and fortune in the city. Each time he introduced the topic, the other boys' answer was the same: "We'll leave next fall, after the crops have been harvested." But when the fall arrived and the crops had been brought in, there was always some other reason not to leave yet.

After a couple of years in Indianola, Riley began to suspect that his friends in the singing group would never leave the farm. As the sultry Delta days passed, he became increasingly restless to play and sing for more people and bigger stakes.

When he reached eighteen in 1943, Riley became eligible for the draft. The United States was at war in Europe and the South Pacific at the time, and more and more young men across the country were being called on for active military service. Riley's boss on the plantation, Johnson Barrett, valued the

Riley believed that the Famous St. John Gospel Singers were good enough to entertain fans in Memphis. When the other group members refused to leave the plantation, however, Riley decided to set out on his own.

young man's work as a tractor driver, and he offered to help Riley apply for an occupational deferment from the draft. Young men who held jobs that were considered essential to their communities were sometimes excused from military service. Barrett persuaded Riley that he would have a better chance of staying out of the military if he were married. Still very much in love, Riley and Martha were eager to start a home together, and on November 26, 1944, the two were married in Indianola.

The following year, Riley served a few months in a military training camp before finally receiving his occupational deferment. According to the terms of the deferment, he was required to remain at his job on the Barrett plantation until the war ended. This restriction made Riley even more restless to leave the Delta and play his music for audiences in the city. When the war finally ended later in the year, he vowed that he would leave Indianola the first chance he got—with or without his friends. When the time to leave the plantation did arrive, however, even Riley was taken by surprise.

Late one evening in May 1946, Riley was pulling Barrett's tractor into the storage shed outside the plantation owner's home. This was a payday, and eager to claim his check, Riley jumped off the vehicle before it had stopped moving. To his amazement, the engine kept chugging without him and the tractor rolled forward against the side of the building. There was only a soft thud when the tractor hit the shed. The machine had been moving very slowly when Riley left it, and it stopped immediately upon impact, without damaging the building. To Riley's horror, it was Johnson Barrett's tractor that had been damaged. The machine's tall exhaust pipe had smashed against the edge of the overhanging roof, and now dangled worthlessly from the vehicle's side.

Johnson Barrett was a fair and honest man. But the tractor was crucial to his work, and Riley knew that Johnson would be furious when he found out what had happened. Riley also knew that his boss would force him to pay for the damages. Faced with the prospect of being saddled with the same type of debt that had ruined his parents' lives, he decided to run away. Without collecting his pay, he rushed home and grabbed his

35

guitar. He persuaded Martha to pack her things and move in temporarily with relatives, until he could afford to send for her. Then he slung his guitar over his shoulder and hiked over to Highway 49. With $2.50 in his pocket, he began to hitchhike north toward Memphis.

Memphis

Memphis in 1946 was an intimidating place for a twenty-year-old farm boy from the Mississippi Delta. Lodged in the southwest corner of Tennessee, immediately bordering on Mississippi to the south and Arkansas to the west, Memphis was the commercial and cultural center of the mid-South. When it came to black music, every successful performer played frequently in the city, and many of the nation's leading jazz, blues, and ragtime musicians actually lived there. Since joining the St. John Gospel Singers three years earlier, King had dreamed of testing his performing skills in front of the city's rowdier and more demanding audiences. But he was totally unprepared for the size and energy of the sprawling southern metropolis.

King had barely set his feet on the Memphis sidewalks before he began asking for directions to Beale Street. A twenty-block stretch of nightclubs, theaters, and cheap hotels, Beale Street boasted some of the best music in the world during the 1930s and 1940s. Each night, crowds lined the street to hear the country's most famous jazz and blues musicians perform. The "Father of the Blues," W. C. Handy, had put the street and its music on the map more than thirty years earlier, and the Club Handy was still one of the neighborhood's leading nightspots.

King knew he had made the right decision in coming to Memphis the moment he saw the Club Handy and the other famous clubs along the street. "I walked down Beale Street and said, 'This is it!'" he remembered years later.[1] Across the street from the Club Handy, he could see the unemployed musicians at Beale Park, where they gathered together each day to talk, play, and sometimes to sleep. Though King never actually made his bed in Beale Park, he did spend a night or two on the floor of an all-night gambling joint and another evening in an empty railroad car before he finally found a place to stay with his uncle Bukka White.

Booker T. Washington "Bukka" White was one of the most gifted composers and guitarists ever to play the blues. He was a master of what is usually known as the "slide" or "bottleneck" technique of playing the guitar. White could make his guitar howl and scream by sliding a small steel or glass pipe up and down the instrument's neck. "The sound seemed to pierce my flesh," Riley would later say of his first exposure to his uncle's style of playing.[2]

Like many blues artists, however, Bukka White had often suffered from terrible misfortune, and he was a sad and bitter middle-aged man when King first encountered him in Memphis in the spring of 1946. During his youth, White had been in a fight in which another man was killed. White always maintained his innocence of the crime, but he fled to Chicago nevertheless. In Chicago, he began to gain attention as a musician—perhaps too much attention for his own good. As the story goes, the Mississippi police arrived in the studio to arrest him just as he was preparing to make his first recording. After serving a backbreaking year at Parchman Farm, the notoriously cruel Mississippi state prison, he was released to resume his career. His music was too complex, however, to become popular among the majority of blues fans. Despite an occasional recording or live performance, he would spend much of his adult life as a farmer and manual laborer.

In spite of his own disappointments in life, White was happy to see his nephew and amused by King's youthful confi-

During his first stay in Memphis in 1946, King stayed with his uncle Booker "Bukka" White. The older man was one of the blues' most innovative guitarists.

dence and enthusiasm. White immediately took the young man in, found him a job, and began to teach him everything he knew about playing the blues guitar. The two men played together every time they had the opportunity. Bukka also lent Riley the money to buy his first electric guitar, a hollow-bodied Gibson. Riley would continue to play the same type of guitar throughout his career.

Curiously, one of Riley's most important innovations on guitar actually resulted from his inability to learn his uncle's style. With a regular guitar, musicians move from one note to the next by shifting their fingers up and down the frets. This means that when a guitarist plays a melodic phrase, each note is clear and distinct. With a slide or bottleneck guitar, however, the musician moves a steel or glass bar along the instrument's neck in a single motion. This style of playing makes it difficult for the listener to tell where one note ends and the next one begins. When the slide technique is used correctly, the guitarist maintains a light but constant pressure on the strings to achieve a vibrating effect, known as a tremolo.

With his huge hands and bulky fingers, however, Riley was never able to master his uncle's style. Instead, he learned to use his powerful fingers to bend the guitar strings as he played each separate note. In this way, he was able to stretch the sound of his guitar notes as he played without using a slide. Over the years, this note-bending technique would become his trademark as a blues guitarist.

King's playing quickly improved. Within a few months, he was good enough to keep up with the older musicians in Beale Park. But informal jam sessions on street corners and in parks with other unemployed musicians were not what King had expected when he left his home for Memphis. He had come here to make a name for himself, and he now realized that he was too young and inexperienced to achieve fame as a musician.

King also felt guilty about the way he had left Indianola—and the people and responsibilities that he had left behind. Martha was still living with relatives and hoping for him to return. He could not yet afford to bring her to the city, and with each of her letters, he felt badly about leaving her alone for such a long time. And there was also the matter of the damaged tractor and the money he owed to Johnson Barrett. The plantation owner had always treated King fairly, and he knew that eventually he would have to repay the debt.

Finally, in March of 1947, Riley grabbed his guitar, said good-bye to his Uncle Bukka, and boarded a bus back to Indianola. He had spent ten long months in Memphis, polishing his skills as a blues singer and guitarist. He knew that he would one day return to the city, but he also knew that he still had a lot to learn.

Back in Indianola, Riley was happy to be reunited with Martha. After ten months, Johnson Barrett's temper had cooled over the tractor accident. King immediately returned to work on the Barrett plantation, where he discovered that he could now command $22.50 a week driving a tractor. With his increased wage and the extra money he earned as a part-time musician, he was gradually able to repay Johnson Barrett for the cost of repairing the tractor. Finally, toward the end of 1948, he headed back north to Memphis. This time, however, he was riding a bus instead of hitchhiking, and his wife Martha was sitting by his side.

The first thing Riley did when he reached Memphis was to catch another bus, across the Mississippi River to West Memphis, Arkansas. He was looking for Rice Miller, known to his fans as Sonny Boy Williamson. Riley had first met Williamson and his musical partner, Robert "Junior" Lockwood, the year before at Johnny Jones' Nightspot in Indianola. The two men had become celebrities together as the hosts of "King Biscuit Time," a popular fifteen-minute radio program broadcast throughout the mid-South each week from station KFFA in Helena, Arkansas. At a time when black music could rarely be found on the airwaves, "King Biscuit Time" featured many of the leading black artists of the day, including Williamson himself on amplified harmonica and Lockwood on electric guitar. When the program was originally aired on November 19, 1941, seven years earlier, it was the first time that most listeners in the Mississippi Delta had ever heard either of the men's instruments played.

By 1948, Williamson had left "King Biscuit Time" and was working in West Memphis as the host of a similar program on radio station KWEM. Riley arrived at the station with his guitar in tow, hoping to audition for a guest appearance on the show.

"I went over and begged him to let me do a tune," King later remembered. "I had my little guitar, and for some reason, he gave me an audition. I sang one of Ivory Joe Hunter's tunes, 'Blues at Sunrise,' and he liked it."[3]

As King would later discover, Williamson had his own reasons for giving the young musician a chance that afternoon. Earlier in the day, the popular radio host had gotten himself into an embarrassing situation, and Riley appeared at the station just in time to help him out. Distracted by his work at the station, Williamson had accidentally agreed to perform at two clubs that night, and he had just noticed that both shows were scheduled for the same time. Williamson decided to let Riley take his place at the lesser-paying engagement, at Miss Annie's 16th Street Grill in the all-black district of West Memphis.

The club's owner, Miss Annie, was a shrewd businesswoman, however, and Williamson knew that she would never agree to let an unknown musician play in her establishment in place of a more popular entertainer like himself. So he decided to make Riley King a household name among the listeners at KWEM—and in a hurry. To Riley's amazement, he was introduced as the program's featured musician that afternoon, performing "Blues at Sunrise" for thousands of African-American listeners across the mid-South.

One of those listeners that day was Miss Annie. She was immediately impressed with what she heard from the young singer/guitarist, and she agreed to let Riley play at her saloon that night in place of Williamson. Unaware of Williamson's predicament, Riley was even more shocked when the older musician informed him that he had already booked him to per-

42

form at a West Memphis club that evening—for the huge sum of twelve dollars!

This was the big break for which Riley had been waiting his entire life. Although he was a bit intimidated by his sudden good fortune, he jumped at the opportunity. "I wasn't about to argue with Sonny Boy," he remembered forty years later. "After all, he let me sing a song, and I thought I was good. I thought I was big stuff then, anyway."

"Don't get me wrong," he continued, "I loved farming life, but getting up at 3:30 or 4:00 in the morning and working till 6:00 or 7:00 in the evening was not something that I really enjoyed doing. I still don't, and to come to a place where I would play one night and get $12.00!"[5]

Riley had never before played in front of a big-city crowd. Despite his confident exterior, he was young and nervous, and his performance that night at Miss Annie's was not one of his best. "My timing was so terrible," he later confessed. "It's not perfect today, but it was really off then." But the youthful crowd at the 16th Street Grill loved every note he played. "The funny thing is," Riley continued with typical humility, "when people are dancing, they don't care how many bars you screw up, as long as you got a good beat."[6] Apparently, Riley had a very good beat that evening. Miss Annie was so impressed that she offered him a regular performance spot at her club—six nights a week for twelve dollars a night plus room and board. There was one condition, however, before Riley could have the position: He would first have to find a job on the radio, like Sonny Boy Williamson.

Miss Annie knew exactly what she was doing by asking King to find his own radio spot. Not only did hosting a radio program enhance a performer's popularity, it also gave him the opportunity to announce—on the air—where he was playing that evening. Miss Annie realized that booking a radio host to perform ensured that her saloon would be filled each night with adoring fans. The only problem for Riley was that Williamson already hosted the most popular program in the area. In Memphis in 1948, there were very few positions available on the radio for young black disc jockeys or musicians.

Riley was determined, however, not to let the opportunity pass. He knew that, across the river in Memphis, radio station WDIA had recently begun to broadcast an all-black music format. In contrast, Williamson's program at KWEM was aired for only fifteen minutes each day. WDIA was the first radio station in the United States to devote its schedule entirely to blues, gospel, and jazz, introduced entirely by black disc jockeys. The station also had a powerful 50,000-watt signal that allowed it to reach one out of every ten black households in the country. Riley hoped that, with all the extra air time, the management at WDIA might be able to squeeze one more musician into their all-black format—even one as young and inexperienced as himself.

It was a rainy, windy afternoon when Riley took the bus across the Mississippi River, and he had a long, wet walk from the bus station to WDIA's studio on 2074 Union Avenue in Memphis. Nervous, frustrated, and soaked to the bone, he looked like anything but the station's next musical sensation when he stumbled through the studio door that afternoon. "I was wearing an old Army jacket," he remembered, "and turned my guitar over on the back so the water would roll over that part of it and not disturb the electronics."[7]

The eager young musician made an immediate impression on the studio staff, but it was not the one he hoped that he would make. "He looked so sad," the station's female program director Chris Spindel would later recall.[8] In fact, Riley looked so sad and pathetic that Spindel and disc jockey Nat Williams, known to his fans as the "Professor," decided to give him a chance. They called in station manager Don Cohen and WDIA's white owner Bert Ferguson, and Riley performed the song he had played for Sonny Boy Williamson the day before. "When he began to play, we all knew he had it," remembered Spindel.[9]

Unfortunately, there were no disc-jockey positions available at WDIA at the time, but the station managers had another idea for Riley. His first job at WDIA was advertising a product called Pepticon, an all-purpose tonic popular among the station's listeners. Each day thousands of people heard him perform the jingle he wrote to promote the product: "Pep-ti-kon sure is good/Pep-ti-kon sure is good/You can get it anywhere in your neighborhood."[10] Although Riley never actually tasted Pepticon, he soon became identified with the tonic in the minds of WDIA's listeners.

> *"I was the first 'Pepticon boy,'" Riley admitted recently. "I don't want to say that too loud. They would send me out on weekends on a trunk [of a car] with some salesmen, and I would play.... They sold a lot of the tonic, and I wondered why people liked it so much until I noticed it was 12 percent alcohol."[11]*

Eventually, one of the disc jockeys at the station resigned, and Riley was offered a job hosting a popular program called the Sepia Swing Club. On the first half of his show, he introduced listeners to new recordings by his favorite blues performers. Each week, he used the remaining fifteen minutes of his show to perform his own compositions, including on-air requests from his fans.

With his popular weekly radio program and his regular sold-out performances at the 16th Street Grill, Riley's reputation grew steadily. The management at WDIA decided that Riley King was too dull and homely a name for such an exciting new radio personality. Soon, Riley was introducing himself on the air as the "Beale Street Blues Boy," after the Memphis musical district that originally attracted him to the city. The name stuck, though it was eventually shortened to "Blues Boy King," and then "B. B. King," by the fans.

B. B. soon became so popular that he was performing regularly in the hottest clubs up and down Beale Street along with his trio from the radio show. Leading blues musicians like Sonny Boy Williamson and Junior Lockwood were happy to play with him. After years of soloing on street corners, B. B. was not accustomed to playing with other musicians, and he sometimes had trouble adjusting his style of performing to the accompaniment of the instruments.

Robert Henry, the owner of the Handy Theater and a number of other Beale Street nightspots, was one of the first people in Memphis to recognize King's talent.

"I was still a very bad musician," he later admitted, "My timing was so bad that in a twelve-bar blues I might play eight bars one time and fifteen the next. But there were a lot of really good musicians in Memphis, and I tried to learn from them. Guys like Hank Crawford, Herman Green, George Coleman, Phineas Newborn—they'd say, 'Look man, here's a pattern; play it like this.' And I'd always listen."[12]

Even as he was struggling to adjust to performing live, B. B. was developing a unique style of guitar that would have a lasting impact on the blues. When he was not performing, B. B. spent hours listening to the recordings of Aaron "T-Bone" Walker, a Texas blues guitarist who had been experimenting for years with the same note-stretching technique B. B. had begun to use. Walker's jazz-influenced "jump blues" had a significant impact on B. B.'s playing during this period. But B. B. was trying to take the electric guitar to a whole different level for the blues.

Jazz musicians like Charlie Christian and the great French Gypsy guitarist Django Reinhardt had already brought the guitar to the front of the jazz ensemble. With the blues, however, the guitar was still used primarily as a rhythm instrument and an accompaniment for the vocalist, with an occasional lead phrase thrown in between the verses. B. B. was among the first blues musicians to make his guitar sing and howl as a lead instrument above the rest of the band. For years, vocalists, like Billie Holliday and Ella Fitzgerald, and saxophonists, like Charlie Parker and Lester Young, had played the leading role in popular American music. B. B. was determined to claim this same leading role for the electric blues guitar. With each awkward performance, he came a little closer to his goal.

After a year with WDIA, B. B. was convinced that the time had come to make his first recording. After months of badgering the station owners, he finally got his chance in 1949. Bert Ferguson contracted the Nashville-based Bullet Recording and Transcription Company to record four songs in the station's Studio A. For the occasion, B. B. chose four of his favorite songs: "Take a Swing with Me," "Miss Martha King," "I've Got the Blues," and "How Do You Feel When Your Baby Packs Up and Goes?" Although B. B.'s vocals on the records were clear and effective, the songs' arrangements were restrained and conservative. The songs did little to demonstrate B. B.'s skills on lead guitar. In fact, the lead performances on "Miss Martha King," the most popular of the cuts, were provided by saxophone and trombone.

The recordings increased B. B.'s popularity in Memphis and throughout the mid-South. The songs enjoyed only a limited release, however, and they did little to establish King as an important new artist for black listeners throughout the rest of the country. Although he often played his own songs live on the air, when it came to promoting his own recordings on his radio show, B. B. turned out to be surprisingly modest.

"I stayed with the station a long time," he later explained, "and quite often would say that I played everything 'from Bing Crosby to B. B.' But I never played my own things. I'd always get one of the other disc jockeys to play them."[13]

Among the people who did appreciate the recordings were Jules, Saul, and Joe Bihari, the Los Angeles–based team of brothers who ran Modern Records. Blues pianist Ike Turner, who would later become famous playing rhythm and blues with his wife, Tina, was working at the time as a talent scout for Modern Records. Turner loved B. B.'s recordings the minute he heard them and sent them on to his employers. The Biharis had a fine ear for the blues, and they immediately signed B. B. to be the first artist to record on their newly formed RPM Records.

The Biharis also contacted Sam Phillips to produce the recordings. A former Memphis disc jockey, Phillips would eventually become one of the most important figures in the history of popular American music. He had recently left his radio job to pursue a career in the recording industry, and he was always on the lookout for local talent. In a few years, he would make his biggest mark on popular music when his Sun Records label introduced the world to the music of Elvis Presley. At the present time, however, Phillips was mainly con-

As WDIA's "Beale Street Blues Boy,"
King became one of Memphis's
most popular radio personalities.

cerned with the blues. He had first listened to B. B. from the roped-off, whites-only sections of the Beale Street blues clubs, and he was eager to work with the talented young guitarist.

The Bihari brothers—especially Jules, who doubled as the producer on many of his most successful early recordings—would play a key role in B. B.'s career. In spite of occasional creative and financial differences, the musician would continue to work with them throughout most of the following decade.

"Often I hear that Ike Turner said he started me out," King explained years later about his initial introduction to the Biharis. "He didn't. But he did get me in touch with the Bihari brothers. Jules Bihari was my man. Jules was like a casino owner [in Las Vegas]—as long as you're doing what you're supposed to do, there was no limit to what he would do [for you]. He couldn't just go into his pockets, but he knew about black music, was a beautiful person, and was just there for you."[14]

During the next few months, King, Phillips, and the Biharis would release a number of singles together on the RPM label. As with the Bullet recordings, the singles generated little interest outside of Memphis and the surrounding area. In Memphis, however, they had a tremendous impact. B. B. was rapidly becoming one of the most popular entertainers in the city.

And outside the city, he was slowly building the network of roadhouses and small blues clubs that would support his highly successful tours in the years ahead. B. B. and his band would venture out a few nights each week to play for rural and small-town audiences in Tennessee, Arkansas, and his native Mississippi. "I would get calls to go to many places to play," said B. B., "and I would go any place where I could get back to Memphis the next day by 8 o'clock."[15]

King would release a number of wonderful recordings for RPM during the next three years, including "She's Dynamite" (1951) and "B. B. Blues" (1951). Even the best of these recordings, however, still featured piano and saxophone in the leading roles, with B. B.'s guitar relegated primarily to the background. King refused to be discouraged, however. He had been working steadily over the years to perfect his approach to electric guitar. He was about to release a record that would finally introduce B. B. King and his unique style of electric guitar to blues fans throughout the country.

Three O'Clock
Blues

The summer of 1951 was an important time for popular American music. A controversy erupted between Sam Phillips and the Bihari brothers that sent the careers of Phillips and B. B. King in two drastically different directions. Phillips was struggling at the time to establish his own Sun Records label as a force in rhythm and blues. He resented that RPM Records had taken such total control over the careers of King and Roscoe Gordon, two artists that he felt he had discovered. Phillips also accused the Biharis of neglecting to pay him for the use of his studio to record King and Gordon.

Phillips knew that he had a hit on his hands when he recorded "Rocket 88" by the Ike Turner Band that June. He was angry with the Biharis, however. And instead of giving the brothers first option on the song, as he usually did, Phillips sold it to Chicago's Chess Records. When the song became a hit— eventually reaching number one on Billboard's rhythm-and-blues charts—the Biharis were furious. They immediately ended their working relationship with Phillips and hired Ike Turner to produce their Memphis recording artists. Turner, it turns out, had left his band shortly before the record was released, and the Bihari brothers did not hold him personally responsible for Phillips's decision to pitch his song to Chess Records.

"Rocket 88" would have a huge impact on the recording industry. Many people consider it to be the first rock-and-roll recording. With its fast, relentless energy, the song would capture the imagination of many young blues musicians, who would abandon the plodding, mournful cadence of the blues for the high-stepping rhythms of rock and roll. King would not be one of them. While more and more of the nation's youth were turning to rock and roll, King became increasingly determined to establish himself as a blues musician.

Ike Turner turned out to be the ideal producer for King's new style of big-guitar blues—especially on the version of Lowell Fulson's "Three O'Clock Blues" that the two men recorded together toward the end of 1951. On the song, the rushed, often blaring arrangements of King's earlier recordings are replaced by a cool, relaxed accompaniment perfectly suited to King's playing. The quartet of drummer Earl Forrest, Johnny Ace on piano, and saxophonists Richard Sanders and Adolph Duncan remain quietly in the background throughout the recording, pushing King's guitar and vocals to the front of the mix. The highlight comes at the middle of the song, where King's traditional verse-ending guitar licks suddenly erupt into a slow, arching solo. In the background, King's voice can be faintly heard, singing along with his guitar.

King's seventh single with RPM Records, "Three O'Clock Blues," was an enormous hit among black audiences all across the country. The song spent several months near the top of Billboard's rhythm-and-blues charts, finally climbing all the way to the number-one spot in February 1952. It would remain at the top of the charts for an incredible fifteen weeks. Five years after he had first arrived in Memphis, King had finally gained a nationwide following. Soon he was receiving requests to play in cities throughout the United States, and many fans—especially on the East Coast—began to complain that they could not receive his radio show. "After 'Three O'Clock Blues,'" he later explained to an interviewer, "I became so popular in a sectional manner of speaking—New York, Washington, D.C., whenever they played their records—that we started taping the

King finally reached number one on the rhythm and blues charts with "Three O'Clock Blues" in February 1952. The song remained at the top of the charts for more than four months.

show."[1] During the next two years, King would release a string of popular singles for RPM Records. Five of these recordings reached the rhythm-and-blues top ten.

In spite of his newfound success, however, King felt increasing pressure to add rock-and-roll numbers to his song list and to adjust his style of playing to suit a younger, and whiter, audience. After Ike Turner's "Rocket 88" exploded on the scene in 1951, rock-and-roll artists like Bill Haley, Chuck Berry, Little Richard, Bo Diddley, and Fats Domino gradually began to dominate the charts. King was never very impressed with the new music, however, or the largely white audience to which it appealed.

"We don't play for white people," he explained during an interview in the 1950s.

Of course, a few whites come to hear us on one-night stands, but they are so few that we never run into segregation problems. I'm not saying that we won't play for whites, because I don't know what the future holds. Records are funny. You aim for the colored market, then suddenly white folks like them, then wham, you got whites in your audiences. That's what happened to Fats Domino, but we don't play rock and roll. Our music is blues, straight from the Delta. I believe we'll make it on that." [2]

Then, in the summer of 1954, something happened that made it impossible for King—or anyone else—to ignore the importance of rock and roll. A young white man from Tupelo, Mississippi, named Elvis Presley, walked into Sam Phillips's Sun Studio to make a recording for his mother's birthday. Presley began jamming with two musicians who had been hanging around the studio that afternoon, bassist Bill Black and guitarist Scotty Moore. The three men quickly came up with a spirited arrangement of Arthur "Big Boy" Crudup's 1946 blues hit, "That's All Right (Mamma)." Impressed with what he heard, Phillips recorded the song on the spot, and popular music was changed forever. Presley's music would not reach the top of the pop charts until 1956, two years later, but no one who heard those original Sun recordings would ever listen to music quite the same way again.

Though the Biharis remained thoroughly committed to recording the blues, King eventually agreed to try his hand at the popular new style of music. "The first rock and roll I ever knew about was Fats Domino and Little Richard," recalled King of some of his earlier attempts to incorporate rock music into his own style of blues. "They were playing blues but differently. I tried to edge a little closer to Fats and all of them, but not to go completely. If somebody bought me a rock-and-roll song...that I thought I could do, I'd try. But it's got to be something I feel comfortable with. I would never do anything I dislike."[3]

On those rare occasions when King did try to fit his music into a rock mold, the result was usually unsuccessful, if not outright embarrassing. "I did once and only once record something as a favor," he later confessed. "One of the Bihari brothers had a friend who wrote a song called, "Bim Bam Boom," and now when I hear it, I still hate it. I did it as a favor, and I'll never do that again."[4]

The growing popularity of rock and roll did nothing to decrease King's success on the road, however. During the period, black blues performers spent most of their time touring the "chitlin circuit." The chitlin circuit was an informal network of small-town bars, roadside nightclubs, and backwoods beer halls that cluttered the sides of highways and gravel roads across the deep South. At most of these places, the price of admission was cheap, and the alcohol was even cheaper. In the notorious barrel houses of the Mississippi Delta, rowdy patrons would actually dip mugs full of whiskey out of an open barrel while the musicians performed from a tiny stage in the rear. The audiences at these tiny, crowded establishments often grew loud and unruly as the night progressed and the liquor poured more freely. Fights were not unusual and lackluster musicians were routinely booed right off the stage, often with bottles and glasses crashing at their feet. It took a brave and gift-

By the early 1950s, King had developed a direct playing
style and a colorful stage presence that could cut through
the chatter and win over the demanding crowds
routinely encountered on the "chitlin' circuit."

ed performer to endure such abuse and to command the crowd's attention. B. B. King was one of the best.

One of King's secrets was the romantic content of his songs. Like most blues singers of the day, he sang primarily about the strained relationships between men and women. From his own broken home as a child, King knew how difficult it could be for a black man and woman to hold a family together amid the economic and social pressures of the Deep South. In song after song, he told the sad, mournful story of broken relationships and broken hearts.

But where many of his male contemporaries wrote angry, mean-spirited songs, portraying women as villains, King usually placed the emphasis on himself and his own pain. He presented himself as a lonely, helpless victim, still carrying a torch for the women who had left him behind. Music critic and blues historian Robert Palmer remembers King once describing the heart of the blues as, "when a man has lost his woman. Which was all he had. He didn't have anything else."[5]

The crowds in the clubs—men and women alike—loved the way that King presented himself as a loser at love. Almost everyone could identify with the sad tales he told, and people would sigh and scream their approval when he offered his hard-earned advice to the audience.

Overcome by temptation or the pressures of work, the men in King's songs had at times acted thoughtlessly, even cruelly, to their loves, and this had cost them dearly. King did not want his fans to make the same mistakes, and he counseled his listeners about love in song after song.

"Ladies," he would begin a typical sermon during an instrumental break in the song, "if you got a man, husband, or whatever you want to call him, and he don't exactly do like you think he should, don't cut him, because you can't raise him over again, you know. Don't hurt him. Treat him nice.

"And, fellas," he would continue for the benefit of his male listeners, "I want to say to you, if you got a woman, a wife, or whatever you want to call her, and she don't do like you think she should, don't go upside her head.... All you [should] do is

58

talk to her softly, real sweet, you know, and you tell her, 'I know you'll do better.'"[6]

Everywhere King performed, listeners found his sad love songs to be irresistible. Unfortunately, King had difficulty applying the message of his songs to his own life. He spent most of his days and nights at work or on the road, and his relationship to his young wife Martha was increasingly strained. When the two did spend time together, they spent most of their time quarreling. Sometimes, King found himself accepting performance engagements simply to escape the pressures at home.

Finally in 1952, Martha King filed for divorce from her husband. The couple had been married for eight years and had no children. King openly reflected on the failed relationship in the song, "Woke Up This Morning," his next single after "Three O'Clock Blues."

King also thrilled his fans on the chitlin circuit by incorporating elements of black worship and gospel music into his blues performances. King had abandoned gospel music for the blues shortly after his first visit to Memphis in 1946. But he would never forget his powerful experiences in the Pentecostal church of his youth—or the lessons he learned watching his uncle Archie Fair lead the congregation.

For one thing, King's clear falsetto singing voice had always sounded more like a gospel shout than a traditional blues howl. For years, he would continue to name gospel artists, such as Dr. Clayton and Samuel McQuery, as his major influences as a vocalist.

Then there were his powerful stage presence and guitar playing. When he was singing or playing guitar, King would often close his eyes and throw back his head in the ecstatic pose of a gospel soloist. He learned to sing duets back and forth with his lead guitar. This "crying counterpoint," as it was sometimes called, successfully mimicked the call-and-response technique used by the minister and the congregation in black Pentecostal worship.

King's phrasing, as a vocalist and a guitarist, was also deeply influenced by the religion of his youth. Like his Uncle

Archie, King would pause suddenly in the middle of a solo or verse, leaving the crowd suspended in a tense, momentary silence before he began to sing or play again. Just as they had done in the Pentecostal services of his childhood, the audiences at his blues performances would gasp together at the sudden stillness, and then roar with approval when the music started again.

King was gradually growing into too large a man to copy his Uncle Archie's habit of stomping up and down and jumping around the stage. But he could still use the strange physical behavior of Pentecostal worshipers to great dramatic effect. One of his favorite tricks was the "blues swoon"—or "going down slow"—in which King would appear to faint dead away, right in the middle of a moving verse or a towering guitar solo. As a child, King had often seen believers who were "slain in the spirit" fall suddenly to the floor during the worship services. He knew how much this behavior excited the other members of the congregation, and he used the same technique to thrill the audiences at his blues performances.

In King's blues concerts, the crowd would gasp as he dropped to his knees. Many concerned fans would rush toward the stage, as the band members helped him to his feet. The crowd screamed words of sympathy and encouragement as he gradually steadied himself and strapped his guitar back over his shoulder. And then the fans would go completely wild when the sound of King's guitar finally began to echo once again throughout the hall.[7]

In the summer of 1952, King got his first chance to test his skills as a performer outside of the Deep South. Impressed with King's recent recording success, Universal Tours, a prestigious New York agency, sent him on a six-month tour of the East Coast. King was sad that the contract required him to trade in his regular touring ensemble for the better-known Tiny Bradshaw Band. But the proposed touring schedule included stops at the Howard Theater in Washington, D.C., the Royal Theater in Baltimore, Maryland, and the legendary Apollo Theatre in Harlem in New York City.

Blues singers like King and Howlin' Wolf (in foreground) entertained audiences with a powerful combination of gospel and the blues. Like King, Wolf was later frequently cited by the young bluesmen of the 1960s as a chief influence.

These three popular concert halls were widely known as the "Big Three Theaters" of the jazz and blues circuits. Playing at any one of them meant that a young artist had finally arrived at the top of the music business, and King was not about to let the opportunity pass. If that was not enough to persuade him, Universal Tours offered the young guitarist the incredible sum of $2,500 a week for his efforts. This was more than one hundred times what King had made driving a tractor on the Barrett plantation less than two years earlier!

King was nervous about playing in front of northern audiences for the first time, but he received plenty of advice from some of the veteran blues musicians in Memphis. He was certain to succeed, they told him, if he continued to perform with the same engaging style he had developed on the chitlin circuit.

"I remember a guy in Memphis telling me," King recently said, "'Now don't you go up there and try to be no Fred Astaire with your top hat, 'cause there's people up there that sweep the floor that can sing better than you'—I'm serious—'and there's cabdrivers that can play better than you. The only thing they can't do is be you. If you be yourself, do what you're known for doing, the people will appreciate you.'"[8]

The Universal tour was a huge success. Audiences in Baltimore, New York City, and Washington, D.C., were as delighted with King's exciting blend of gospel and the blues as his regular fans in Memphis and the Mississippi Delta. Soon King was receiving more invitations to perform than he could possibly accept. With the money from the Universal tour, he assembled a large road crew and performing ensemble, bought a first-class touring bus, and began to spend more and more of his time on the road.

More than anything else, King loved the excitement of touring clubs across the country and the thrill of a live performance in front of a totally new audience. Life on the road also had its disadvantages, however. According to King's biographer, Charles Sawyer, the band's one-night stands were sometimes as far as 800 miles (1,280 km) apart.[9] The band would play until the early hours of the morning and then drag themselves onto the bus for a full day of traveling. They caught what

King poses with fellow performers, including Big Mama Thorton (with maracas), backstage at a Memphis club during the early 1950s.

sleep they could during the day on the bus, often arriving just in time to set up for the evening's performance.

The worst problem for the band, however, was the constant threat of violence that they faced on the road, in the crowded nightclubs and beer halls where they performed each night. Throughout his early career, King and his companions on the road displayed an uncanny ability for attracting danger. The tour bus was involved in several serious accidents during the early 1950s, and riots, fights, and fires seemed to follow the band everywhere they went. At one point, things got so bad that the band members began to carry guns to protect themselves from hostile audiences.

The most frightening encounter with an angry crowd occurred in Houston in 1956. In between sets, King lingered in the crowd after the other band members went backstage, to chat with an attractive young admirer from the audience. Standing back in the crowd, the girl's boyfriend grew angrier and angrier as he watched the two talking onstage.

When the set resumed, the man dashed across the stage and pulled the piano bench out from under King as the musician prepared to take a seat. As King fell to the floor, there was an angry face-off between the band members and several of the boyfriend's companions from the crowd. Luckily, things quickly calmed down, and the band was able to complete the set and leave the building without any further incidents.

Many people in the angry Texas crowd were still holding a grudge, however. When King and the band attempted to pull away from the club in their tour bus, members of the mob opened fire on them with guns they had been concealing in their coats. Instinctively, the band members pulled out their own weapons and began to shoot back at the crowd as the bus sped away. Fortunately, no one was actually hit by the sudden spray of gunfire. The tour bus was riddled with bullet holes, however, and King imposed a permanent ban on band members carrying guns on the road.

For King, however, the rewards of touring more than compensated for all the hardships and risks. For several years, he tried to balance his growing live performance schedule with his responsibilities at WDIA. By 1953, however, touring had simply become too big a part of his life to leave time for his work as a disc jockey. He left the station to devote himself full-time to the road. Though he did not realize it at the time, King's departure from WDIA would also represent the end of his recording career in Memphis. "Boogie Woogie Woman," a rollicking number recorded with Ike Turner in September of 1952, would be King's final Memphis-produced release.

During the mid-1950s, he often averaged more than 300 performances a year, the majority of them one-night stands. The work was hard and the schedule was often grueling. As a for-

During the 1950s, King kept up such a grueling
schedule that his touring bus became his second home.
He sometimes spent as many as three hundred days
a year performing on the road.

mer Mississippi sharecropper, however, King had endured his fair share of hard work and grueling schedules.

> *"The early days of touring was kind of like being on the plantation,"* he explained years later to an interviewer. *"There wasn't 'no' or 'if I want to' or 'maybe.' You had to do it. If you lived on a plantation, it was expected of you to be up at a certain time in the morning, to do your chores and everything. So naturally you went ahead and did what was necessary.*
>
> *"Well, it was the same thing in this kind of music for a long, long time,"* he continued. *"Just having a good record wasn't good enough. I found that if I played Las Vegas or Memphis or wherever, my record sales would almost double in that area. I also noticed that I got press that I didn't get prior to playing there. People now call from all over the world wanting to do interviews. But years ago, that didn't happen. Did not happen. So we had no other way of exposing ourselves, and I got used to it."*[10]

Life on the road was hard work, but King found that the rewards could be phenomenal. In 1954, King earned an estimated $480,000 from touring alone, a figure that made him one of the highest-paid performers in the world—black or white.

Live at the Regal

B. B. King's contract with RPM Records finally expired toward the end of 1958. Despite his long-standing loyalty to the Bihari brothers, especially Jules, King had been considering moving to another record label for some time. Over the years, King had become one of the top-selling blues recording artists in the country, and he was becoming increasingly dissatisfied with the way the Bihari brothers were treating him and handling his career.

For one thing, the Bihari brothers paid him much less per record sold than he felt he could be receiving from one of the major recording labels. A number of his friends, like Fats Domino and Ray Charles, had recently signed with larger companies, and King was jealous of the larger paychecks that they were already receiving. There were other factors to consider, as well. Earlier in the year, King's touring bus, Big Red, had been destroyed in a terrible traffic accident, and he badly needed the extra money to cover the debt.

An even worse problem for King was the Bihari brothers' practice of adding a second name to the copyright of the guitarist's compositions. On many of his hits during the period, such as "Three O'Clock Blues" and "Rock Me Baby," fictional characters like Jules Taub and Joe Josea were listed as cowriters.

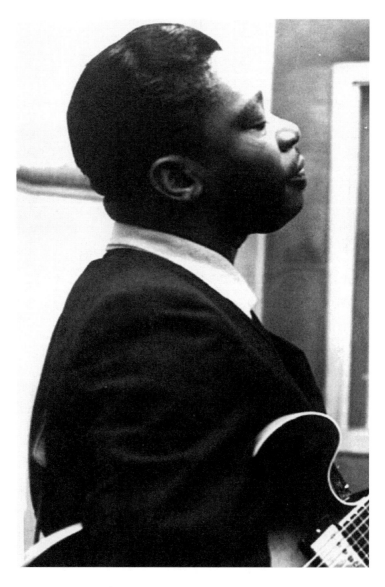

By the end of the 1950s, King's accomplishments in
the recording studio had finally begun to match the
quality of his live performances, and his performances
began to get more frequent radio airplay.

This meant that King was forced to share with the Bihari brothers half of the writer's royalties for songs that he had actually written by himself. Many black composers and recording artists of the day were forced to settle for these types of deals with their recording labels and music publishers. King felt that the arrangement was unfair and dishonest, however, and he decided to find a better deal elsewhere.

There were other problems with the way the Bihari brothers were managing King's recording career, however. In order to compete with the major labels, the Bihari brothers sold their albums for $.99 to $1.99 a copy, in contrast to the $3.99 to $4.99 charged by the larger companies. Since King's royalties were based on a percentage of the actual price, he often received less than half of what artists with major labels received for the same amount of work and with the same level of popularity.

Years later, King reflected on his decision to part ways with his original label.

> "I told the Biharis that I was going to leave them because they were selling albums for $.99, I believe it was," he explained. "We never got credit for any work we did, never listed in Billboard. That made me feel bad. I felt that I did pretty good work from time to time, but I wasn't making any money."[1]

Even with his problems at RPM, King was still making plenty of money on the road, however. During the late 1950s, he put almost all of his energy into touring. With all the time he spent on the road, it took him almost two years to find the right label. He recorded briefly with Chicago's Chess Records, including the single "Recession Blues." Meanwhile, the Bihari brothers were desperate to keep King on their roster, and they persuaded him to record a number of additional songs for RPM between 1959 and 1961. King refused to sign another long-term contract with his old label, however.

King's singles for RPM during the period included a number of unusually upbeat, big-band-style arrangements. His 1961 release of Duke Ellington's "Don't Get Around Much Anymore" features the eighteen-piece Duke Ellington Orchestra. King sounds much more like a Las Vegas crooner on the recording than a dedicated blues artist.

Finally toward the end of 1961, King signed with ABC-Paramount Records. The label had made their fortune during the late 1950s by recording white, middle-of-the-road pop singers like Paul Anka and Steve Lawrence. Like almost every other major label at the time, however, the executives at ABC-Paramount were determined to take advantage of the exciting new music being made by black artists. They had recently signed Fats Domino and Ray Charles to long-term contracts.

It was Fats Domino, in fact, who persuaded King to sign with ABC. The popular New Orleans rhythm-and-blues musician had just settled a lucrative deal with the company, and he wanted King to get a piece of the action. "We got a big company that believes in you," Domino told King at the time, "got somebody in there you can work with, won't put you on the shelf. They're not only in New York and Los Angeles, but they got distributors around the world. You need that."[2]

As he had hoped, King made a lot of money during his years with ABC-Paramount. The label offered him $25,000 just for signing his contract, and his singles consistently sold between 50,000 and 100,000 copies. His 1964 release "How Blue Can You Get?" was his first single to reach Billboard's hot 100, peaking on the pop charts at number 97.

> *"ABC offered me a good contract," he explained years later, "and that was the first time I started to see real money. If we sold a hundred thousand copies with the Biharis, that was considered a hit. A hundred thousand copies with ABC was just a normal release. I felt and still do today that a big company can do a lot more for you, and they were so big then."* [3]

The soulful Ray Charles was one of the first black rhythm and blues singers to have wide public appeal. King hoped that by signing with ABC-Paramount he would be able to attain the success already enjoyed by black vocalists such as Charles and Fats Domino.

For all the studio's vast financial resources, however, the management at ABC-Paramount understood very little about King's music. Admittedly, the Biharis never paid King adequately for his work, but they knew exactly what he needed in order to recreate the appeal of his live performances in the recording studio. King's records with RPM are among the best of his career.

From the beginning, ABC-Paramount tried to sell King to white record buyers as a traditional pop singer, in the mold of Sammy Davis, Jr., or Tony Bennett. The big bands, backgrounds choruses, and lavish, full-scale production on 1964's "Help the Poor" and "Stop Leadin' Me On" might have worked perfectly for some of ABC's other recording artists. King, however, sounded uncomfortable and completely lost in the mix of his ABC-Paramount recordings. He was making more money than he ever had before, but he soon began to realize that the quality of his music was suffering at the new studio. For the first time in his career, King gradually began to lose interest in his work.

King's live performances also began to suffer during the early 1960s. Convinced that he needed to play for larger audiences in bigger concert halls, King changed to Shaw's Booking Agency of New York City in 1960. The new agency offered King the promise of greater national exposure by booking him as the opening act for more established mainstream artists—like Jackie Wilson, Lloyd Price and Sam Cooke.

King hoped that these performances would allow him to introduce his music to a whole new generation of fans. The move backfired, however. Increasingly, young black fans wanted to hear music that sounded more contemporary and middle class. Many of these younger fans were embarrassed by King's flamboyant, gospel-inspired renditions of the blues, which they associated with ignorance and poverty.

King was absolutely miserable during many of these performances. At times, he and his band were actually heckled and booed by audiences who were impatient to hear the more mainstream acts on the bill.

"It really hurts me to hear the blues put down," he complained to journalist Charles Keil at the time. "It's our big contribution—something to be proud of. Some people don't want to lower themselves to listen, or they think they're lowering themselves if they listen; they're afraid of what people will say.

"There have been times," he continued, "when I go out to sing and give it all I have—people just sit there, chin resting on one hand, staring into space. I mean they couldn't care less. When that happens, sometimes I walk off and cry. I'm serious—I really do cry. It's emotionally upsetting to see people hate my music who should like it." [4]

If many black fans had lost interest in the blues, however, a new generation of white fans was getting ready to take their place. In cities like Chicago, New York, and Boston, a new breed of young white rock-and-roll musicians were discovering the richness and vitality of the blues. Mike Bloomfield, Al Kooper, Elvin Bishop, and Paul Butterfield were among the emerging artists whose music was clearly inspired by the likes of King, Muddy Waters, and John Lee Hooker.

After the arrival of the Beatles in New York in 1964, a number of successful groups from England—like the Animals, the Yardbirds and the Rolling Stones—introduced listeners in the United States to their own unique form of blues-inspired rock and roll. Within a few years, musicians like Jimi Hendrix, Johnny Winter, Janis Joplin, and Cream would be taking a fairly straight rendition of the blues to the top of the popular charts.

Perhaps the most lavish in their praise for King were the two young white American blues guitarists Elvin Bishop and Mike Bloomfield. King's biographer, Charles Sawyer, reports that whenever either of the two were asked how they learned to play the blues, they would always give the same answer:

"By copying B. B.'s licks."

"B. B. who?" the confused interviewer would inevitably ask. "The real monster, B. B. King!" Bishop and Bloomfield would respond.[5]

The enthusiasm of young white musicians revitalized the careers of many of King's peers from the chitlin circuit. By the mid-1960s, Muddy Waters, Howlin' Wolf, and John Lee Hooker were appearing regularly on college campuses and at regional folk festivals. For some reason, however, King's more flamboyant, gospel-inspired approach to the blues was slower to gain a following among white teenage fans. Rock-and-roll musicians from both sides of the Atlantic went out of their way to sing King's praises, but white audiences and record buyers still needed to be convinced.

Still, King played for white audiences whenever he got the chance, and as the 1960s progressed, he slowly began to develop a following. "We have mostly Negro adults at our gigs," said King in the mid-1960s, "but I've noticed in the last year or so I've had a lot more of the white kids come in than ever before."[6] It would be a few more years, however, before King would finally begin to establish himself as a mainstream musician with mainstream appeal, with equal popularity among black and white fans.

During the mid-1960s, the civil rights movement inspired a number of books about traditional black music and the blues. The most important of these books were *Blues People* by the black poet and playwright Leroi Jones and Charles Keil's *Urban Blues*. Keil's book provided the most thorough and insightful descriptions ever given of the work of major blues artists such as Muddy Waters, John Lee Hooker and Bobby "Blue" Bland. At the center of the book was a lengthy profile of and interview with B. B. King.

"B. B. King," wrote Keil at the time, "is the only straight blues singer in America with a large, adult, nationwide, and almost entirely Negro audience. If the adjectives 'unique,' 'pure,' and 'authentic' apply to any blues singer alive today, they certainly apply to B. B. King."[7]

Urban Blues celebrated the blues as a serious and important form of traditional American music. It also introduced King and his music to thousands of readers who had never heard of him before. Just as Elvis Presley was the "King of Rock and Roll" and James Brown was the "Godfather of Soul," B. B. King had suddenly come to be regarded as the "King of the Blues."

King continued to be discouraged, however, by his failure among young black audiences and the poor quality of most of his recordings for ABC-Paramount. At one point during the mid-1960s, he became so depressed that he stopped practicing his guitar altogether.

In 1965, King celebrated his fortieth birthday on a sour note. His expensive tour bus had recently been stolen, and his second marriage was in serious trouble.

King had met Sue Carol Hall following a performance in his hometown of Indianola, Mississippi, early in 1958. The couple were married that summer, and Sue—unlike King's first wife Martha—traveled frequently with B. B. and took an active interest in her husband's career. Sue also wanted to become more involved in King's business dealings. B. B. had always been free and careless with his money, however, and he did not want his wife telling him how to run his career.

For years, Sue accepted B. B.'s refusal to listen to her advice. When he began to experience serious financial difficulties in the mid-1960s, however, the marriage began to come apart. Sue filed for and obtained a divorce in 1966. Just as with King's first marriage, the couple were married for eight years and had no children.

King himself was not childless, however. During the 1950s, between his two marriages, he had openly acknowledged fathering eight children with women he had met while touring.[8] Throughout the 1950s and 1960s, King spent almost all his time on the road, and he had no real home to share with his children. But he knew what it was like to grow up in poverty, and he assumed full financial responsibility for all of his children, including providing a college education for those who wanted it. King's daughter Shirley was actually raised by his father Albert, along with the rest of his family on a farm outside of Memphis.

In spite of King's artistic difficulties with ABC-Paramount, the label did provide him and his fans with one bright spot in 1965. Recorded at Chicago's Regal Theater in November of 1964, *Live at the Regal* presents King in a classic live performance with a small touring ensemble. Thirty years later, it remains one of the most highly acclaimed live blues recordings ever produced and possibly the finest release of King's career.

> *"I don't know why 'Live at the Regal' came out so special,"* King later reflected. *"It seemed like everything was right. [Arranger-producer] Johnny Pate set up everything, making sure that we had good sound, and the audience was good.... At the Regal, and in Chicago, they still think well of and respect me and the dignity of the Blues, thanks to Muddy Waters and the rest.... That particular day in Chicago everything came together and the audience was right in sync."*[9]

The sad truth, however, was that the Regal Theater in Chicago was one of the few places in the country where King could still play to such an approving audience. With his failed marriage and stalled career, the only thing that kept King playing during this period was sheer determination. After all, he had already survived the backbreaking existence of life on a Delta plantation. He knew that if he worked hard and trusted his instincts, eventually things would improve.

In the mid-1960s, he added to his live performances a song that perfectly expressed the toll that the last few years had taken on his personal life and his career. The song was Ray Hawkins's 1958 rhythm-and-blues hit "The Thrill Is Gone." In concert, King performed the heartbreaking song with so much conviction that many in the audience were moved to tears.

For several years, King had wanted to record the song as a single. He had tried several times in the past, but he could never find an arrangement that would allow him to capture the

76

song's mournful intensity in the recording studio. Though he knew the song could be a huge success, King was determined not to release it until he got it right.

A few more years would pass before King would finally find the right studio arrangement for "The Thrill Is Gone." When he finally did release the song, however, it would change his career forever.

The Odd Couple

In 1966, King hired Sidney Seidenberg to handle his business affairs. After years of sloppy bookkeeping and bad financial advice, King had little money to show for all his years of touring and recording. He had also recently been saddled with additional debts from his failed marriage and the loss of his touring bus. He badly needed someone to balance his books and put his financial records in order, and Seidenberg turned out to be the ideal person for the job.

A flamboyant, cigar-chomping character, Seidenberg had recently abandoned a successful career as a New York City accountant to try his hand at the music business. Years later, Seidenberg would insist that he had never intended to enter the management end of the business; he was always content simply to handle his artists' books and other financial dealings. When King offered him the opportunity to take full control of his career in 1966, however, Seidenberg jumped at the chance. Before he would accept the job, however, Seidenberg presented King with a couple of ground rules.

His first rule was that King's career would be handled with the same efficiency and advance planning with which Seidenberg would approach any other business. "One of the things I did as an accountant," Seidenberg later explained, "is

King achieved his greatest success after he hired businessman and promoter Sidney Seidenberg to manage his career.

plan, and I told B. B. about five-year plans, and goal-setting, which is how we still work today. Right from the start, I tried to work on new things for him to broaden his career and stretch his talent."[1]

Seidenberg was also determined to ensure that he was adequately compensated for his services. He was prepared to make a lot of money for his client, but King had to be willing to pay for it. "For every million you make," he told King at the time, "I'll get a hundred grand."[2] After years of struggling to make it on the plantation and on the road, this was exactly the kind of reasoning that King understood and appreciated, and the two men worked well together from the start.

As enthusiastic as he was about taking the job, Seidenberg quickly discovered that managing King's career was no easy task. "[B. B.] had no market," he later recalled. "Blues wasn't even considered good enough for the rhythm-and-blues spots." [3]

Seidenberg's first challenge as King's manager was to confront the recording executives at ABC-Paramount. He renegotiated a five-year contract for his client, persuading the record company to help him promote King's music outside of the blues and rhythm-and-blues markets. With the extra money and control that Seidenberg secured from ABC, King was suddenly able to make better recordings and book better venues for his performances.

The move paid off almost overnight when King's single, "Don't Answer the Door, Part One," became a huge rhythm-and-blues hit toward the end of 1966. The song was a classic blues performance reminiscent of King's best work from the 1950s. It abandoned the large brass ensembles that had been cluttering most of his recordings with ABC in favor of a simple blues quartet of guitar, drums, bass, and organ. Peaking at number two on the rhythm-and-blues charts, "Don't Answer the Door" was King's first top-ten recording in more than five years.

The albums that King released during his early years under Seidenberg's management were also among the best of his career. 1967's *Blues Is King*, along with *Lucille* and *Blues on Top*, both released in 1968, present King at the top of his form. His guitar work was clearer and more inspired than it had sounded in years. And he was also beginning to sound as if he were enjoying himself—something even the best of his recordings had lacked since the late 1950s.

On the title cut to *Lucille*, King finally got the chance to share with the fans of his recordings the same offbeat love story with which he had been delighting concertgoers for years. Since his early days on the chitlin circuit, fans everywhere had demanded to hear the tale of how King first named his trusted guitar, Lucille.

King's uncle Bukka White gave him the money to buy his first guitar in 1946, during the young musician's first trip to Memphis. The model King chose was an amplified, hollow-bodied Gibson. As King now tells the story, it was love at first sight. The instrument provided him with just the sound that he had been searching for. It gave his solos a crisp, piercing quality, and his chords the rich, full sound of an acoustic guitar. Over the past fifty years, King has bought more than fifteen new guitars, all of them customized to meet his needs. Each one of them has been a hollow-bodied Gibson named Lucille.

As much as King loved his first guitar, it would be more than a year before he gave the instrument a name. A number of stories have circulated over the years about how Lucille first received her name. The most popular one involves a particularly rowdy night at a tiny bar in Arkansas, where King and his band were playing during the winter of 1949.

On the song, "Lucille" (Bluesway, 1968), recorded live in Los Angeles in December of 1967, King tells the story in the crowd-teasing style of a black Pentecostal minister. He punctuates each sentence with an inspired burst from his guitar and leaves plenty of time between phrases for the audience to scream and shout their approval. And using a vocal technique that has long been one of his trademarks, he even begins the song with a stutter borrowed from his childhood.

> *"The way...the way...the way I came by the name of Lucille," he says as the crowd begins to roar. "I was in Twist, Arkansas. (I know you've never heard of that.)"*
>
> *King pauses for a moment to let the crowd quiet down, playing his guitar quietly in the background. "And one night," he suddenly continues his story, "the guys started a brawl over there, started brawling. And the guy that was with his old lady, when she fell over on this gas tank that was burning for heat, the gas ran all over the floor."*

For some fifty years, King has performed with a black, double-cutaway, semihollow electric guitar he refers to as "Lucille." Made by the Gibson company, the guitar has a bright but woody sound, well suited to the blues.

*King plays a huge burst of guitar to match the sud-
den gasp from the crowd.*

*"And when the gas ran all over the floor," he con-
tinues with a mixture of comedy and drama, "the
building caught on fire and almost burned me up trying to save Lucille."*

*Again, the crowd roars while King delivers anoth-
er loud phrase on guitar.*

*"Oh," he stops suddenly in the middle of his play-
ing, as if he had actually forgotten to tell the best part
of the story. "I imagine you're still wondering why I
called it Lucille."*

*He strikes another loud round of notes as some
people in the crowd begin to laugh.*

*"The lady that started that brawl that night was
named Lucille," he says with a smile in his voice.
King's guitar rings clearly above the audience's
laughter.*

*"And that's been Lucille ever since to me. One
more now, Lucille," he adds, quickly introducing the
crowd to his guitar and the huge solo that follows
before they have the chance to respond again.*[4]

In concert, King often attributed magical powers to his
instrument, including the frequent habit of saving his life. In one
often repeated episode, King and his guitar were both thrown
from his automobile in a terrible accident on the highway. After
the initial crash, the car rolled over and over toward King, who
lay helpless and bleeding by the side of the road. King would
have certainly been crushed under the vehicle, he claimed, if it
had not been for Lucille. As the car approached him, the guitar
suddenly turned up on its side and lodged itself beneath one of
the car's front wheels, just as it was about to fall on top of him.[5]

Over the years, Lucille has become such a popular part of
King's performance that he now has to carry more than one guitar with him on tour. The problem is, overzealous fans will sometimes steal the instrument as a souvenir, right off the stage or out
of King's dressing room.

"The last time," he recently recalled with typical good humor, "somebody went in that next room and got it. But luckily the sheriff was able to find it. A young fella had taken it home, and the funny thing was, when the sheriff came up to his house, he said, 'Oh, did you come for the guitar?' [Laughs.] Yeah, that was the last time, but I've got about five or six of the Lucille model at this time."[6]

Partly in response to Seidenberg's urging, ABC created its Bluesway label late in 1966. Designed to feature its growing roster of blues artists, the label would survive only until 1970, but King would provide it with its most commercially and critically successful recordings. The first of these was 1968's "Paying the Cost to the Boss," which reached number 10 on the rhythm-and-blues charts and number 39 on the pop charts. The second successful release for Bluesway was "The Thrill Is Gone," the song that would change King's career.

"I had been carrying 'The Thrill Is Gone' for years," he later explained of the recording session on which he finally found the right formula for the song. "Had tried it many times, but it would never come out like I wanted it. That night, though, it seemed just right. We were in the studio from about 10 o'clock to 2:30, 3:00 in the morning. The funny thing was, producer Bill Szymczyk didn't like it at first, didn't care for it at all. Anyway, we finished and went home. About five in the morning, Bill calls me and says, 'I've got this idea to put strings on 'Thrill,' and I said fine.... It really enhanced it."[7]

With its perfect blend of classic blues and a lush string arrangement, "The Thrill Is Gone" finally produced a sound that allowed King to stay true to his roots and appeal to a more mainstream audience. The song quickly vaulted to number three on the rhythm-and-blues charts. Even more important for King's career, it peaked at number 15 on Billboard's hot 100, giving King regular airplay everywhere and his first real exposure to a nationwide audience.

With the release of "The Thrill Is Gone," B. B. King was suddenly a household name throughout the United States. At the end of the year, King received his first Grammy Award, as the Academy of Recording Arts and Sciences named "The Thrill Is Gone" the top rhythm-and-blues recording of the year.

After "The Thrill Is Gone," King's next three singles placed in the top 20 on Billboard's rhythm-and-blues charts. Two of them, "Ask Me No Questions" and "Chains and Things," actually crashed the top 50 on the pop charts.

Meanwhile, Sidney Seidenberg was hard at work behind the scenes. He arranged for King to perform as a headliner at many of the most popular rock-and-roll venues in the country, including several sold-out performances at the Fillmore East in New York City. At the first Fillmore performance, guitarist Mike Bloomfield introduced King to the crowd as "the greatest living blues guitarist."[8] After hearing King perform, there were few in the audience who would disagree.

In the summer of 1969, King went on tour with the Rolling Stones, proudly introducing the Delta blues to the more than 1 million fans who had paid to see the British rock group. This time, however, there were few people in the audience who were yawning or booing his performance. The success of blues-rock guitarists like Eric Clapton, Duane Allman, and Jimi Hendrix had prepared most rock-and-roll fans for King's style of blues. At every city along the tour, fans sat mesmerized to hear B. B. play his guitar.

Seidenberg also booked King at clubs and concert halls frequented by older audiences. With the assistance of his friend Frank Sinatra, King became a big hit at many Las Vegas supper clubs during the late 1960s, at the same moment he was beginning to find acceptance among the younger rock-and-roll fans. "They have a lot of rooms in Vegas that need a lot of talent," recalled Seidenberg, "and we got in there by promising

Mick Jagger and guitarist Keith Richard of the Rolling Stones perform in 1969. King's appearances with the British rock and roll band that summer marked his successful debut with white rock-and-roll fans.

to work for very little money on the basis of 'Give us a chance; if we do good—keep us.' One of our earliest shots came when Sinatra was working the main room at Caesar's [Palace], and we were working the lounge. Sinatra's people had to okay it, which they did because they all like B. B."⁹

Following the success of "The Thrill Is Gone" in 1970, everyone wanted King to perform. Less than five years into his five-year plan, Seidenberg had helped King climb all the way to the top of the music business. Early in 1970, King became the first blues artist ever to appear with Johnny Carson on "The Tonight Show." And then in October of 1970, he appeared as a guest on "The Ed Sullivan Show," performing "How Blue Can You Get?" live in front of more than 70 million viewers across the country. The popular Sunday-night variety series had earlier launched the careers of both Elvis Presley and the Beatles in the United States. A guest spot on the program was a sure sign that an artist had reached the big time. King was forty-five years old, with twenty-five years of performing behind him, and he had finally begun to achieve the recognition and respect that he had been seeking for himself and the blues.

One of King's most interesting projects during this period was the album, *Indianola, Mississippi Seeds* (Harmony, 1970). Released toward the end of 1970, the recording featured collaborations between King and several popular rock-and-roll artists of the day, including Leon Russell, Carole King, and Joe Walsh. The album's production was softer than the production used on King's regular blues recordings, and his singing and playing were much more restrained. Most of the songs worked surprisingly well, however, demonstrating for a younger, mostly white audience King's powerful influence on the younger rock-and-roll musicians.

Several songs from the recording were released as singles, including "Hummingbird" and the popular "Chains and Things" (ABC, 1970). The highlight, however, was the album's sad but hilarious version of "Nobody Loves Me But My Mother (And She Could Be Jivin' Too)." King had recorded the song alone during a break in the sessions, accompanying himself on the piano while the other musicians were relaxing in the next room. Producer Bill Szymczyk persuaded King to include the song on the album with no additional accompaniment. King's quiet, raw performance stands in powerful contrast to the louder, more spirited playing that fills out the rest of the recording. "Sure, I can play rock and roll along with the best of them," King seems to be saying as he crouches over the piano, "but the blues is still what I'm all about."

Never Make Your Move Too Soon

" t is astounding that B. B. King has never been to Europe,"
wrote Charles Keil in Urban Blues.[1] By the time Keil's book
was published in 1966, blues singers Howlin' Wolf,
Muddy Waters, and John Lee Hooker had already begun to
delight audiences in European cities such as London, England;
Paris, France; and Hamburg, Germany. King, however, had
yet to cross the Atlantic Ocean at the time, and millions of
potential European fans had never heard his name.

In 1971, Seidenberg finally persuaded ABC to send
King to London. The trip was the final stage in Seidenberg's
first five-year plan for King, and he hoped it would help the
musician build on the recent string of successes begun with
"The Thrill Is Gone" and the 1969 Rolling Stones tour.

The ten days that King spent in London gave him the
chance to reunite with the Rolling Stones and some of the other
young British rock-and-rollers who claimed him as an influence.
Among the European musicians with whom King recorded during his brief stay in London were Gary Wright, Klaus Voorman
of the Plastic Ono Band, and the Beatles' Ringo Starr. The 1971
LP, *B. B. King in London*, featured several songs from these sessions, including a wonderful duet between King and popular

British blues singer Alexis Korner. Breaking a long-standing tradition, King played acoustic guitar on some of the London sessions, the first time that he had played the instrument in public in more than twenty-five years.

The London trip was the beginning of King's lifelong passion for traveling abroad. Over the next few years, he would play for thousands of new fans throughout Europe, Africa, Asia, and Latin America. "I've found what going out of the country meant," King would later explain. "I realized there was more of a market than I thought in every country I went to. We carried the blues to places it had never been, and I started to feel like an ambassador of goodwill and music, especially the blues." [2]

The highlight for King was his highly publicized tour of the Soviet Union at the close of the decade. The communist nation had long been closed to rock-and-roll and blues musicians from the West, and King took great pride in helping to break the barriers down and bring the blues to a nation full of people who would certainly know how to appreciate it. "You know," he would later boast to an interviewer, "we were in the Soviet Union in '79, way before perestroika."[3]

King enjoyed the hit singles, television appearances, and overseas tours. He had worked hard for more than a quarter of a century to earn all the recognition, and he seemed happy and relaxed in the midst of his newfound fame. King's first love, however, was performing on the road—in the bars, supper clubs, and small concert halls where he had first perfected his style. After several successive singles failed to make the Billboard charts toward the end of 1971, King concentrated more and more of his time and energy on touring the blues circuit. "When I didn't tour regularly," he later explained, "record sales stood still, and I would see that attendance wouldn't be what it was."[4]

King's determination to spend most of his time on the road caused a major disagreement between the musician and his flamboyant manager. One of Seidenberg's first achievements when he took over King's career in 1967 was to persuade his

By the early 1970s, King and his band were making frequent television appearances. Here, he plays for the TV cameras and the studio audience of the extremely popular "Ed Sullivan Show" in October 1971.

star to get rid of his cherished touring bus. Seidenberg felt that King spent far too much time touring small clubs and halls. He could better serve his career by devoting himself to interviews, television appearances, and other forms of national and international publicity.

Over the years, Seidenberg had used his success with King to build a large roster of talented young recording artists whom he represented, including the popular rhythm-and-blues group Gladys Knight and the Pips. When King began to disregard his advice and resumed a full-time touring schedule, Seidenberg began to spend more and more of his time with his other clients, especially Gladys Knight.

King resented all the attention that Seidenberg was now devoting to other performers—especially when the Pips began to top the pop charts in the early 1970s. By the end of 1973, the two men were barely speaking to each other. The following year, they officially ended their professional relationship.

"I don't know why he has that bus now," Seidenberg said in frustration a few years after the split. "Maybe it's ego; maybe it's his return to familiar things. The first thing I did when I took over was to get him to get rid of the bus. The first thing he did when he went on his own was to buy another bus. Right away it broke down; he had to get a new engine."[5]

Following the break with Seidenberg, King experimented briefly with the smooth, lushly produced style of soul music popularized by Al Green, Stevie Wonder, and Marvin Gaye. The 1973 album, *To Know You Is To Love You* (ABC), included a collaboration between King and the song's composer Stevie Wonder, who played keyboard on several of the cuts. The album also featured the legendary Memphis Horns, who provided the background for a number of classic soul ballads during the period.

In the early 1970s, King used his newfound popularity to establish the Foundation for Inmate Rehabilitation and

King performs at a prison during the 1970s. Out of a deep caring for those gone astray, King has played free concerts for thousands of inmates in dozens of prisons across the United States.

Recreation (FAIRR) along with lawyer F. Lee Bailey. Over the years, King has performed for the inmates in more than forty U.S. prisons, releasing live albums based on two of his more recent performances at San Quentin.

In the mid-1970s, King got the chance to record with his old friend Bobby "Blue" Bland. Robert Calvin Bland had first met King in Memphis in the late 1940s. As a teenager, he played rhythm guitar in one of King's early quartets at the 16th Street Grill.

Over the years, the two men had remained admirers and close friends. But they had always recorded for competing music labels, and had consequently never been able to make a recording together. In 1973, however, King's recording company, ABC, purchased the Duke and Peacock labels on which Bland released all his records. The two men soon began touring the country together, and in 1976, they jointly released two albums, *Together for the First Time* and *Bobby Bland and B. B. King Together Again...Live.* The highlight of the two recordings was the live album's rollicking version of "Let the Good Times Roll," recorded live in Los Angeles in 1976.

"Bobby Bland and I had wanted to do something together for a long time," King later explained. "Bobby, to me, is one of the greatest singers in the blues field, one of the greatest all-around singers.... Whatever he does, blues or otherwise, it's good."[6]

As King later recalled, the only remaining obstacle to the collaboration was Bland's obstinate fear of flying on airplanes. "I don't remember who suggested [doing an album together]," said King with a laugh, "but I remember that Bobby don't like to fly, and to do the album he had to fly. I remember telling him that the same God up there that he believes in so much is down here and on planes, too. He cussed me out and came anyway."[7]

Later in the decade, King finally tried his hand at jazz when he made a series of recordings with Joe Sample and the Jazz Crusaders. King had always resented the way that many jazz fans and musicians looked down on the blues, and spoke out against this injustice whenever he got the chance.

> *"When I go to a jazz club," he had complained to Charles Keil in the mid-1960s, "sometimes the leader or the [master of ceremonies] will say, 'B. B. King, the well-known blues singer, is in the audience tonight.' And the way he says 'blues' you know he really means 'nasty." I believe that if you're doing something as well as you can, working to improve, people shouldn't put you down. There's no reason why a man can't sing the blues as a profession and still be a gentleman. That's the main reason I'm sticking to the blues, because I'd like to show people that it can be done."* [8]

In spite of his anger over this unfair treatment, however, King had never abandoned his appreciation for jazz. In interviews, he consistently listed saxophonist Lester Young and guitarist Charlie Christian among his major influences.[9] And he also tried to keep up with the latest jazz trends and recordings.

King had always admired the way the Crusaders incorporated elements of gospel and the blues into their cool instrumental performances and recordings. When ABC acquired the group's Blue Thumb label in the late 1970s, King approached the band's leader and keyboardist Joe Sample about the possibility of making a record together. King and the Crusaders recorded together on the album *Midnight Believer* (ABC, 1977), with the guitarist skillfully blending his classic blues playing into the band's slick, upbeat arrangements. A single from the recording, "Never Make Your Move Too Soon," was one of King's biggest hits from the period, rising to number 20 on the rhythm-and-blues charts.

Whenever King got the chance, however, he preferred to play the blues, and he managed to record one classic LP during the period, 1975's *Lucille Talks Back* (ABC). Without Seidenberg to talk him out of it, King decided to try his hand at producing the album, a task he had never before attempted. Surprisingly, the album represented an impressive debut for King as a producer. It was widely praised, even by those who had begun to resent King's frequent crossovers into soul, rock and roll, and popular ballads. "When it comes to a blues album," he said somewhat defensively at the time," I think I'm qualified to say what's good, and what isn't."[10]

King continued to have his critics, however, as his success outside of the blues circuit inevitably caused resentment among some of his less commercially successful peers. One of the most wounding remarks came from King's old friend Muddy Waters. The Chicago-based guitarist had been one of the first blues musicians to benefit from the blues revival of the early 1960s. But his record sales had suffered in the mid-1970s, when young fans increasingly abandoned big-guitar rock and roll in favor of soul, disco, and punk rock.

"Now B. B. King plays blues," Waters said during the late 1970s to interviewer Robert Palmer, "but his blues is not as deep as my blues. He plays a type of blues that can work in a higher class place, like to a higher class of peoples—they call 'em urban blues."[11] Given King's experience throughout much of the 1960s, Water's comments must have been doubly wounding.

King recently commented on the criticism he received during this period.

> "It's really strange," he told an interviewer, "that the same folks who support you when you're struggling, turn their backs on you or start running you down when you've gotten somewhere. They feel it's some kind of betrayal, but I'm the one who feels betrayed. That just doesn't seem like a good reason. It's not fair to me. Why would you support somebody only when they're struggling and not be happy for them when they've made it? You can't stand still."[12]

In 1978, King and manager Sidney Seidenberg were reunited. The simple reason for both men was money. King's excessive touring had once again left him in debt. Seidenberg had recently lost the successful Gladys Knight as a client, and he was once again looking for a new act to represent.

> *"The consensus in the industry is that it was a mistake for me to take B. B. on again," Seidenberg told King's biographer Charles Sawyer at the time. "People say, 'Why do you want to start over again with a man his age? The blues market is cold now.' But I think I can heat him up again. He's got as much potential now as in 1968, when I first took him over. He's still got appeal for college kids. The college kids that are grown up now—they'll still buy his records provided he's promoted properly."[13]*

Seidenberg wasted little time taking control of King's career. He encouraged his star to reduce his time on the blues circuit and concentrate instead on the jazz-blues collaborations he had begun with the Jazz Crusaders. A second King-Crusaders project, *Take It On Home* (MCA), followed in 1979, along with a string of other jazz-oriented collaborations for King.

Among the best of these jazz-blues recordings were the 1981 single, "There Must Be a Better World Somewhere," with King playing alongside pianist Mac "Dr. John" Rebbenack and saxophonists Hank Crawford and David "Fathead" Newman, and the 1982 "Blues 'n' Jazz" set. Produced by Seidenberg himself, the recording was one of the most successful attempts ever to blend these two important forms of traditional American music. King gave one of the finest performances on the record on "Blues 'n' Jazz," sharing the limelight with jazz trumpeter Woody Shaw and Memphis saxophonist Fred Ford.

Seidenberg also encouraged King to begin composing soundtracks for feature films during this period. Watching movies has always been one of King's favorite ways to relax, and he is always particularly attentive to the music used in film soundtracks. King's home is filled with endless piles of videos—

hundreds and hundreds of them—and he frequently carries a VCR with him when he is traveling on the road. Even with King's enthusiasm to compose for motion pictures, however, it took a while for him and Seidenberg to find the right project. In 1985, King finally got his chance to work as a movie composer on director John Landis's *Into the Night.*

"I had been a little sad because they didn't use me in *The Blues Brothers,*" he told interviewer Colin Escott a few years later. "Then someone called and said that John Landis wants to see me. That felt like meeting [the great film director] Cecil B. DeMille to me. I was timid in speaking to him and in a way of speaking, I was almost saying, 'Why me?' He just finally told me, 'I like your guitar sound, so I'd like to use you on the film.'"[14]

Even with Landis's encouragement, King still balked at the idea of providing the soundtrack for the movie, warning Landis that he had no previous experience with formal composition. Landis was unperturbed, however. He worked out a system where King could simply play his guitar in response to the action on the screen.

"They put the scenes up without music," King recalled later, "and I would play—like those keyboard players for the silent movies."[15] King's performances were recorded as he played. Another composer then charted what King had played and synced it to the film.

King continued to compose for motion pictures throughout the remainder of the decade. Unfortunately, some of the projects, like *Amazon Women on the Moon* and *Thieves Like Us*, were not exactly the type of films to inspire his best work.

King's involvement with *Thieves Like Us* did give the musician his first chance to act, however. He was on the screen for only a moment, reciting the single line, "Would you like a Pepsi?"

Still, it was quite an experience for a former sharecropper from Itta Bena, Mississippi. "I can remember it now," he said a few years later with a laugh. "I guess I should—one line!"

Even with his budding film career, King continued to spend much of his time on the road. Increasingly, his live shows were packed with white fans, even in the clubs along the blues circuit that he favored when touring. Many of these fans still remembered King from his greatest years of success during the early 1970s, and they yelled out for his big hit, "The Thrill Is Gone," whenever there was a lull in the performance.

"If I didn't sing that song," he joked with a reporter a few years later, "they'd probably throw a tomato at me!"[16]

When Love Comes to Town

On September 16, 1985, B. B. King celebrated his sixtieth birthday the same way he had celebrated almost every one of his birthdays during the previous forty years—on the road. After all the years of recording and performing, he still spent between 200 and 300 days a year on the blues and supper-club circuit, and at 60, he showed very little sign of slowing down.

By this time, King and Seidenberg had finally reached a compromise about the musician's lifelong addiction to touring. According to the agreement, King could tour the blues circuit as often as he liked, as long as he reserved a sufficient amount of time to participate in the other tours, public appearances, and promotional activities arranged by Seidenberg. "The way B. B. travels and performs is much the same as that of a Barnum and Bailey Circus," Seidenberg told an interviewer with a sigh of resignation, "running around the country but in a logical manner."[1]

Over the years, King had more than kept his half of the bargain. Since his first trip to London in 1971, he had performed in fifty-seven countries on five continents, including well-publicized visits to the Soviet Union and Japan. King was always thrilled about the enthusiastic response he received from fans at concerts and blues festivals abroad. But it continued to frustrate him that he sometimes found audiences in the United States—especially some young black fans—to be less receptive to the blues.

> *"When I played around the country," he complained to an interviewer, "quite often I would hear a young black that will come up to me and say, 'Oh, I'm only 18 years old and I don't know anything about the blues.' But, then [here I am] playing for whites—kids from 8 to 80. Maybe I'm being a little hard or harsh, but I'm thinking that the people that are in the blues field that I am—we owe young blacks the knowledge of the origin of this kind of music and what it has stood for and what it has meant to us through the years—and what it did for the world at large."[2]*

With this in mind, King has increasingly come to regard himself as a crusader for the blues. He devotes more and more of his time to special projects designed to promote the blues and to educate young people about the music and its rich heritage. Easily the most impressive of these events was June 1988's Chicago Blues Festival, where King led an all-star cast of blues performers in front of more than 250,000 fans. In the early 1990s, he also played a leading role in a series of blues festivals sponsored by Benson and Hedges. Along with King, the concerts featured Buddy Guy, John Lee Hooker, Al Green, the Staple Singers, and King's old friend and touring partner Bobby "Blue" Bland.

In 1993, King followed up on the momentum from the Benson and Hedges festivals with *Blues Summit* (MCA), a star-studded blues album that may be the most accomplished recording of his career. On the recording, King shares the studio with leading blues guitarists John Lee Hooker, Albert Collins, Buddy Guy, and Robert Cray, and vocalists Koko Taylor and Etta James. King's explosive duet with Hooker on "You Shook Me" is one of the most powerful blues recordings ever made, an opinion shared by music critics around the country. *"Blues Summit* is quite simply the best B. B. King album in 20 years," wrote Down Beat's Bill Milkowski shortly after the album was released.[3]

In addition to his collaborations with leading blues musicians, King continued to share the stage and the recording studio with other types of musicians during the late 1980s and early 1990s. These double bills made Seidenberg happy, since they expanded King's audience and broadened his appeal. The collaborative performances also made King happy since they gave him the chance to play the blues for people who might never have heard the music before.

In the spring of 1986, King shared the bill in a series of performances with the legendary jazz trumpeter Miles Davis. Both in their early sixties, the two men began their careers in the late 1940s, and both had been credited with inventing a new style of American music. For King, it was the gospel-influenced, guitar-oriented urban blues developed during his years on the chitlin circuit. For Davis, it was the cool style of jazz known as bebop. For many listeners, the two men and their respective styles of playing represented the opposite extremes of contemporary black music.

Though the two aging stars did not actually play together during the program, fans everywhere were delighted to hear performances by the undisputed masters of jazz and the blues in the same place on the same evening. The two men's drastically different stage styles spoke volumes about the differences between their respective musical traditions.

Elegantly dressed in a black tuxedo, King put every ounce of his huge body into pleasing the crowd. Like the gospel worshipers of his youth, he stomped his feet, pounded his fist into his hand, and even fell to his knees during the performance.

Davis, on the other hand, was dressed much more casually, in a loose sweater and slacks. True to the cool, disinterested style of jazz that he helped to invent, the trumpeter played many of his solos with his back to the audience. And when he was not playing along with his large ensemble, he frequently wandered aimlessly around the stage or disappeared behind the curtains to the side.

In spite of the many differences, however, both men had tremendous respect for each other's musical talents, and their performances were among the finest of their careers. "It is obvious," wrote Rolling Stone critic David Fricke, "that for [King] the thrill of playing the blues is hardly gone."[4]

King's most successful collaboration during the 1980s, however, was the highly proclaimed pairing of the blues guitarist and the Irish rock quartet, U2. In the summer of 1988, King had just finished a sold-out performance in Dublin, Ireland, when the Irish band's lead singer, Bono, and guitarist, the Edge, knocked on his dressing-room door. During a brief conversation, the two young rock stars showered the older blues artist with compliments.

"When they got ready to leave," King later recalled, "I said to Bono, 'You know sometimes when you're writing, would you write one for me?'"[5] The Irish rocker politely agreed and then left the room.

The following year, Seidenberg called King with the news that Bono had, in fact, kept his promise and written King a song. Showing real insight into King's music, Bono had penned a stunning blend of gospel and the blues called "When Love Comes to Town."

"[Seidenberg] said they were gonna be playing in Fort Worth," King later explained, "and I could open the show for them, too. Then I found out that he had wrote the song not for me, but us to sing together. Anyway, we rehearsed it, and that night I came back for the finale and he and I sang 'When Love Comes to Town.' Forty thousand people stood up. Forty thousand people!"[5]

The Bono–King duet had an impact far beyond the capacity crowd in Fort Worth, however. The original live performance of the hit single became a part of "Rattle and Hum," the name of both a live album and a feature film documenting the band's 1989 United States tour. Along with their inspired performance in front of the Texas fans, Bono and King are

103

King receives an honorary doctorate from Rhodes College in Memphis in 1992. By that point he had already received several, including one from Boston's prestigious Berklee School of Music for life achievement.

shown in the film rehearsing the song in the empty coliseum earlier in the day. King continued to travel with the band throughout the tour, including a special New Year's Eve performance in Dublin.

Even King's biggest fans were surprised by the song's success, particularly the powerful vocal exchange between the two men. "I was prepared to hear some great blues guitar," U2's guitarist the Edge would later confess of his first exposure to King's singing, "but I was not prepared to hear a voice like that. We were blown away!"[6]

In 1985, King received one of his many honorary doctorates when the prestigious Berklee College of Music in Boston presented him with a degree for "life achievement." King had received his first honorary degree from Yale University in 1977, and he always found the academic honors to be an emotional and humbling experience for a man who had dropped out of school after the tenth grade.

Addressing the entire Berklee student body, King instructed the youngsters not to let "the blues" stand in the way of their goals in life. "I saw many closed doors," he said in his address, sounding remarkably like his own grade school teacher, Luther Henson. "I stumbled, but those doors never moved me. You have to try and try again to keep it going."[7]

As he approaches the final years of his career, education has begun to play a bigger and bigger role in King's life.

"People have asked me," he reported in 1992, "if you could do it again, what would you change? The thing I would change is, I would finish high school. I only went through the tenth grade. I would also go to college [and] learn more about music.... I think the schooling would have changed my playing for the better."[8]

King believes it is especially important for young black people to receive a good education. In many ways, he believes, the failure of many young people to appreciate the blues reflects an overall ignorance of history. "More than anything else," he said in a recent interview, "it's important to study, to know history. To be a black person and sing the blues, you are black twice. I've heard it said, 'If we don't know from whence we came, we don't know how to go where we are trying to go.'"[9]

King has no plans to retire from touring in the foreseeable future. When he does eventually park his tour bus permanently, however, he plans to spend much of his time with young people, teaching students at black high schools and college campuses about African-American history and the blues. "I want to sit down with the students, play a little, and explain what this music is all about and what it has meant to us over the years."[10]

King has already begun to get a head start on his plan to become involved in children's education. In the past few years, he has made numerous appearances on "Sesame Street" and other innovative projects for the Children's Television Workshop. In the summer of 1993, he and country singer Johnny Cash became the first two performers to contribute to a series of book-cassettes for children. On his cassette, *Rainy Day Blues*, King sings and narrates an original story about a rained-out baseball game.

Over the years, King has managed to remain surprisingly successful at avoiding political themes in his music or in his onstage banter. Even on the most obvious exception, 1964's "Help the Poor" (ABC), King shifts the song quickly from the poor and homeless to his own sad condition as a brokenhearted lover. Almost all of his songs are about love, shattered relationships, and the unquenchable drive to set things right—and not political or social causes.

King has always been socially committed off the stage, however. In addition to his work with prisoners and in education, he has for years been an active supporter of his friend Charles Evers. Evers is a progressive Mississippi politician and brother of the slain 1960s civil rights activist, Medgar Evers. But while King has frequently held concerts to raise money for both Evers and other progressive politicians over the years, he has refused to use his stage as a platform to promote their political ideas.

In the late 1980s, many of King's friends and admirers were disturbed by the blues artist's budding friendship with Lee Atwater, the chairman of the Republican National Committee and a close adviser to George Bush. Both Atwater and Bush were avid blues fans, and Atwater could actually hold his own as a guitarist among his famous musician friends on the blues circuit.

106

After Bush was elected president in 1988, King began to receive regular invitations to the White House. King and Atwater played together frequently, in and out of the White House. And on one well-publicized occasion, King visited Bush in the Oval Office, presenting the president with an authentic version of one of his customized Lucille guitars.

One of the people who was most confused by King's association with Atwater and Bush was his old friend Charles Evers. Evers wondered how King could lend his support to the leaders of a conservative political party that voted consistently against the interests of black people.

"Charles is my good friend," King told Rolling Stone when he was asked about Evers's comments. "But his political beliefs and all that—that's his. The same thing with Mr. Atwater. I don't let nobody tell me who I can speak to or who I can be friends with—that's one good thing about this country.[11]

"Out of all the parties and all the people and all of the rhetoric," he continued in defense of his White House appearances, "out of all the many things people have said and done, nobody has taken any interest in B. B. King as far as the White House is concerned until Lee Atwater and the president of the United States, Mr. Bush."[12] King had waited his entire life for the recognition he had recently received, and he was determined not to let anything spoil it for him or his music—including a difference in political beliefs.

In addition to politics, relationships also continued to take a backseat to the blues for King. According to recent estimates, King has thirteen children—five of them adopted—and anywhere from fourteen to twenty-three grandchildren.[13] Over the years, he has taken an increasingly active role in the lives of his children, financing their college educations and encouraging the show-business careers of two of his older daughters, Claudette and Shirley. The years of constant traveling have kept him apart from his family most of the time, however. In interview after interview, he now openly acknowledges that this is one of the few regrets of his life.

"I've never been the father I wish I could have been and wanted to be," he recently confessed sadly. "Due to my job, I

King poses with his daughter, Barbara, and granddaughter in a photo taken in 1984.

was just never there in person. In spirit, yes, and financially, yes. [But] I've been told by my children that just being there in person would have been better."[14]

After two failed marriages, King seems to have accepted the fact that full-time touring and a successful marriage simply do not mix. He now admits that it is unfair to expect a woman to marry a man who is always away from home on the road—although some of the women he knows do not seem to agree. "It really hurts me," he told an interviewer recently, "when a

In the early 1990s, King endorsed Gibson's "Blues King," an acoustic guitar well-suited to delta-style playing. King, who has played Gibson guitars throughout his career, has also endorsed a Gibson model styled after the original "Lucille" and bearing his name.

lady says, 'We've been to dinner three times. What are your intentions? I had one lady say, 'If you're not ready, I'm gonna get married [to someone else].' So I said, 'Go ahead. I'll bring my guitar and play at your wedding.'"[15]

In 1995, King was approaching his seventieth birthday and more than a quarter of a century as a bachelor. He recently joked with an interviewer that he plans to marry a younger woman "in five years or so."[16] But it seems unlikely that he will ever marry again, at least as long as he continues his full-time career.

The early 1990s were among the most commercially and critically successful of King's career. In addition to the duet with Bono and the highly acclaimed *Blues Summit* LP, he released a number of fine recordings. Among the highlights were the spirited duet with blues singer Bonnie Raitt on Dr. John's "Right Time, Wrong Place" (MCA, 1991) and a new collaboration with Joe Sample and the Crusaders on "I'm Moving On" (MCA, 1991). He also completed a new round of recording sessions in London in 1991, playing an inspired lead guitar on Gary Moore's "Since I Met You Baby," from the British artist's recent Christmas album, *After Hours* (Virgin Records).

King has now spent almost half a century as a blues musician. Though he is now at the top of the entertainment business, things have not always been easy for him. For years, he endured both the neglect of the white community and the ridicule of many black fans. His contribution to the blues now appears to be beyond dispute, however, as well as his position as one of the towering figures of popular American music. Each year, the awards and honors continue to accumulate.

In 1987, he was awarded the Grammy Lifetime Achievement Award. In 1990, he received a star on Hollywood's Walk of Fame and the Presidential Medal of Honor, the highest honor that can be awarded to a civilian in this country. The following year, he was the recipient of a prestigious National Heritage Fellowship.

A founding member of Memphis's Blues Foundation, King was also recently honored when the award given to the winner of the foundation's annual National Blues Amateur Contest was named after his legendary guitar. Each year, talented young guitarists from all over the world compete in Memphis for the coveted Lucille Award.

In the summer of 1992, King's current label, MCA Records, paid the artist a huge tribute with the release of a four-disc, seventy-seven-song boxed set of his music. The recording spans King's entire career as a blues musician, from his earliest hits, "Miss Martha King" and "Three O'Clock Blues," to his more sophisticated work in the early 1990s. Critics proclaimed the package to be one of the most substantial bodies of work ever produced by a blues artist.

Even more than the personal acclaim, King takes pride in the impact that his recent success has had on the reputation of the blues. Everywhere that he performs these days, he has noticed that more and more music fans—particularly younger black listeners—are beginning to treat the traditional music of the Mississippi Delta with respect.

> "This may sound weird," he told an interviewer," but I am now starting to get just a little of the sweetness that comes when black kids look at me sometimes and say, 'Hi, Mr. King!' That makes me feel very good.
>
> "And quite often now," he continued, "I'm starting to have black kids come up to me and want an autograph, not saying, 'You might as well give me one since you gave that other guy one.' I'm starting to hear them say, 'May I have your autograph and not for my mother or my grandmother or my uncle or my grandfather—but for me.'"[17]

Throughout his career, B. B. King has remained remarkably faithful to his roots in the blues. He uses each new project and each new performance to enrich his understanding of what the blues are and what they can become. For King, the secret has always been to find the music's authentic sound—like the

Now in his fifth decade as an entertainer, King plays
with more power and sweetness than ever in his career.
With each note he coaxes from "Lucille," King, like
few others, continues the rich American musical
tradition known as the blues.

heart-wrenching sounds he heard from black singers in both the Pentecostal churches and beer halls of his youth.

"Forty-one years," he told an interviewer in 1992, "and I'm still looking for that sound. I wouldn't know it if I see it, but if I heard it, I got it. I've been searching for this sound all the time, and I still don't have it."[18]

For millions of listeners around the world, King and his music have come to embody the very thing for which he continues to search—the authentic sound of the blues.

Chronology

September 16, 1925: Born in Itta Bena, Mississippi, the
  son of sharecroppers
1929 Moves to Indianola with his mother, leaving his
  father behind
1934 King's mother dies
1944 Marries Martha Denton
1946 Wrecks Johnson Barrett's tractor and moves to
  Memphis
1947 Returns to Mississippi Delta
1948 Back in Memphis; plays on Sonny Boy
  Williamson's radio program on KWEM; becomes
  Pepticon Boy for WDIA
1949 Records "Miss Martha King" and meets the Bihari
  brothers
1951 Records "Three O'Clock Blues" for Modern
  Records
1952 "Three O'Clock Blues" reaches number one on
  Billboard's rhythm-and-blues charts; divorced from
  Martha King; goes on first tour of the East Coast
1958 Marries Sue Carol Hall
1961 Signs contract with ABC-Paramount
1965 Release of Live at the Regal

1966 Publication of Charles Keil's *Urban Blues*; divorced from Sue Carol King
1967 Sidney Seidenberg becomes King's manager
1969 Tours with the Rolling Stones
1970 Releases "The Thrill Is Gone," which reaches number 15 on Billboard's hot 100; appearances on "The Tonight Show" and "The Ed Sullivan Show"
1971 First trip to London
1976 Touring and recording with Bobby "Blue" Bland
1979 Tours Soviet Union
1985 Composes first film score, for John Landis's *Into the Night*
1986 Performs on same bill with Miles Davis
1987 Receives Grammy Lifetime Achievement Award
1988 Headlines in front of 250,000 fans at the Chicago Blues Festival
1989 Records "When Love Comes to Town" with Bono and U2
1990 Receives Presidential Medal of Honor and star on Hollywood's Walk of Fame
1991 Receives National Heritage Fellowship; named Down Beat's rhythm-and-blues artist of the year
1992 Headlines at Benson and Hedges Blues Festival
1993 Releases critically acclaimed *Blues Summit*
1994 MCA Records releases the four-record boxed set, *B. B. King: King of the Blues*

Source Notes

CHAPTER 1

1. *New York Times*, January 15, 1992, C1.
2. *Esquire*, June 1986, 263.
3. *Jet*, February 24, 1986, 42.
4. *Rolling Stone*, November 30, 1989, 90.
5. Charles Sawyer, *The Arrival of B. B. King* (New York: DaCapo Press, 1981), 95, 106.
6. *Jet*, February 24, 1986, 60.
7. *Down Beat*, February 1992, 17.
8. *Rolling Stone*, November 30, 1989, 93.
9. Stanley Booth, *Rhythm Oil: A Journey Through the Music of the American South* (New York: Vintage Books, 1991), 105.

CHAPTER 2

1. Larry Cohn, ed., *Nothing But the Blues* (New York: Abbeville Press, 1993), 35–36.
2. Stanley Booth, *Rhythm Oil: A Journey Through the Music of the American South* (New York: Vintage Books, 1991), 98.

3. Colin Escott and Andy MacKaie, "An Interview with B. B. King," from *King of the Blues* (New York: MCA Records, 1992), 41.
4. Ibid.
5. Ibid.
6. Ibid., 42.

CHAPTER 3

1. Colin Escott and Andy MacKaie, "An Interview with B. B. King," from *King of the Blues* (New York: MCA Records, 1992), 42.
2. Charles Sawyer, *The Arrival of B. B. King* (New York: Da Capo Press, 1981), 158.
3. Escott, 42.
4. Ibid., 46.
5. Ibid.
6. Ibid.
7. Ibid., 46–47.
8. Larry Cohn, ed., *Nothing But the Blues* (New York: Abbeville Press, 1993), 195.
9. Ibid.
10. Escott, 51.
11. Ibid.
12. Stanley Booth, *Rhythm Oil: A Journey Through the Music of the American South* (New York: Vintage Books, 1991), 101.
13. Escott, 51.
14. Ibid.
15. Ibid.

CHAPTER 4

1. Colin Escott and Andy MacKaie, "An Interview with B. B.King," from *King of the Blues* (New York: MCA Records, 1992), 51–52.
2. Ibid., 17.

3. Ibid., 53–54.
4. Ibid., 54.
5. Robert Palmer, *Deep Blues: A Musical and Cultural History of the Mississippi Delta* (New York: Penguin Books, 1981), 56.
6. Charles Keil, *Urban Blues* (Chicago: The University of Chicago Press, 1966), 98.
7. Ibid., 184.
8. Rolling Stone, November 30, 1988, 92.
9. Charles Sawyer, *The Arrival of B. B. King* (New York: Da Capo Press, 1981), 73.
10. Escott, 58–59.

CHAPTER 5

1. Colin Escott and Andy MacKaie, "An Interview with B. B. King," from *King of the Blues* (New York: MCA Records, 1992), 54.
2. Ibid.
3. Ibid.
4. Charles Keil, *Urban Blues* (Chicago: University of Chicago Press, 1966), 109.
5. Charles Sawyer, *The Arrival of B. B. King* (New York: Da Capo Press, 1981), 94–95.
6. Escott, 21.
7. Keil, 102.
8. Sawyer, 77.
9. Escott, 57.

CHAPTER 6

1. Charles Sawyer, *The Arrival of B. B. King* (New York: Da Capo Press, 1981), 25.
2. Colin Escott and Andy MacKaie, "An Interview with B. B. King," from *King of the Blues* (New York: MCA Records, 1992), 25.
3. Ibid.

4. B. B. King, "Lucille," Bluesway Records, 1968.
5. Ibid.
6. *Guitar Player*, June 1992, 80.
7. Escott, 57.
8. Sawyer, 106.
9. Ibid., 26.

CHAPTER 7

1. Charles Keil, *Urban Blues* (Chicago: University of Chicago Press, 1966), 102.
2. Colin Escott and Andy MacKaie, "An Interview with B. B. King," from *King of the Blues* (New York: MCA Records, 1992), 62.
3. Ibid.
4. Charles Sawyer, *The Arrival of B. B. King* (New York: Da Capo Press, 1981), 62.
5. Ibid., 22.
6. Escott, 58.
7. Ibid.
8. Keil, 106.
9. Sawyer, 154.
10. Escott, 34.
11. Robert Palmer, *Deep Blues: A Musical and Cultural History of the Mississippi Delta* (New York: Penguin Books, 1981), 260.
12. *Down Beat*, February 1992, 17.
13. Sawyer, 20.
14. Escott, 37.
15. Ibid.
16. *Ebony*, February 1992, 44.

CHAPTER 8

1. *Jet*, February 24, 1986, 61.
2. Ibid., 61–62.
3. *Down Beat*, December 1993, 47.

4. *Rolling Stone*, May 22, 1986, 22.
5. Colin Escott and Andy MacKaie, "An Interview with B. B. King," from *King of the Blues* (New York: MCA Records, 1992), 37.
6. *Rolling Stone*, November 30, 1989, 90.
7. *Jet*, June 17, 1985, 22.
8. Escott, 63.
9. *Ebony*, February 1992, 46.
10. Ibid., 47.
11. *Rolling Stone*, November 30, 1989, 90.
12. Ibid., 92.
13. *Ebony*, February 1992, 46; *Rolling Stone*, November 30, 1989, 87.
14. *Ebony*, February 1992, 46.
15. *Jet*, November 11, 1991, 18.
16. *Ebony*, February 1992, 45.
17. *Jet*, February 24, 1986, 63.
18. Escott, 63.

Selected Bibliography

Booth, Stanley. *Rhythm Oil: A Journey Through the Music of the American South*. New York: Vintage Books, 1991.

Charters, Samuel. *The Legacy of the Blues*. New York: Da Capo Press, 1977.

Cohn, Lawrence, ed. *Nothing But the Blues*. New York: Abbeville Press, 1993.

Evans, David. *Big Road Blues: Tradition and Creativity in the Folk Blues*. Berkeley: University of California Press, 1982.

Jones, Leroi. *Blues People*. New York: Morrow, Quill Paperbacks, 1963.

Keil, Charles. *Urban Blues*. Chicago: University of Chicago Press, 1966.

Marcus, Greil. *Mystery Train: Images of America in Rock 'n' Roll Music*. New York: Penguin Books, 1991.

Palmer, Robert. Deep Blues: *A Musical and Cultural History of the Mississippi Delta*. New York: Penguin Books, 1981.

Sawyer, Charles. *The Arrival of B. B. King*. New York: Da Capo Press, 1981.

Index

Page numbers in *italics* refer to illustrations.

About the Author

David Shirley is a freelance writer living in Brooklyn, New York. In addition to his book *A Good Death*, he has written numerous books for children and young adults. His writings on popular music have appeared in *Option*, *Rolling Stone*, *Spin*, *Chicago Review*, *Raygun*, and *New York Press*.